D Nathanson
717-683-4860

A SELF-HELP MEMOIR

The Anatomy of a Yenta

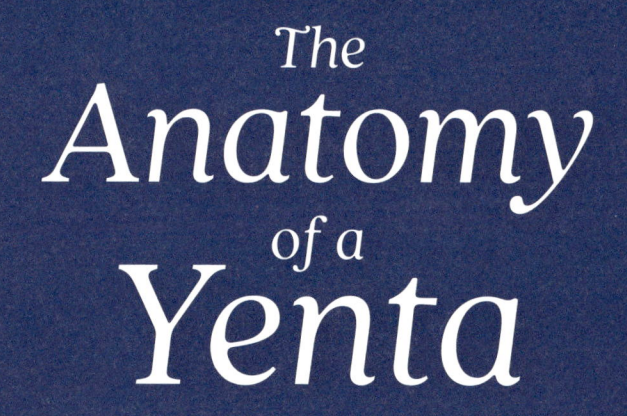

Break the Yenta Mold,
Embrace Dignity,
& Create an Elegant Life

RAIZY FRIED

THE ANATOMY OF A YENTA

The Anatomy of a Yenta
Copyright © 2024 by Raizy Fried
All rights reserved

No part of this book may be reproduced in any form, photocopy, electronic media or otherwise without written permission from the copyright holder.

Published by:
RAIZY FRIED PUBLISHING
Lakewood, NJ 08701
www.raizyfried.com

Printed in Turkey

Available for purchase online at:
www.raizyfried.com

Distributed by:
NIGUN DISTRIBUTION
4116 13th Ave.
Brooklyn NY 11219
718-977-5700

We welcome all questions and comments
info@raizyfried.com

Written by: Raizy Fried
Editor: Elky Langer
Proofreader: Andrea Kahn
Graphic Design and Layout: Shani Jay Creative

ISBN 978-0-57896698-4
First Edition: November 2024

DEDICATION

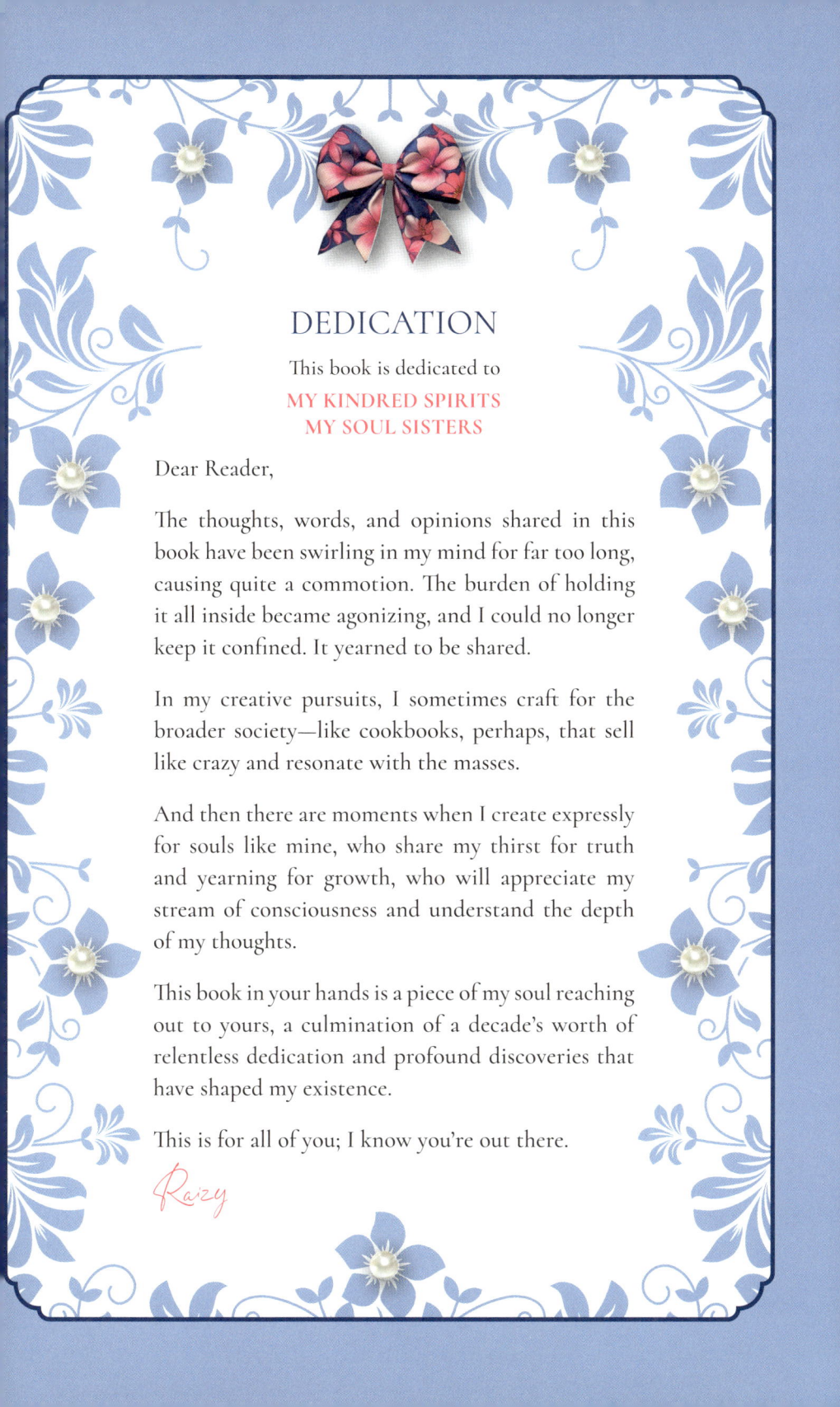

This book is dedicated to
**MY KINDRED SPIRITS
MY SOUL SISTERS**

Dear Reader,

The thoughts, words, and opinions shared in this book have been swirling in my mind for far too long, causing quite a commotion. The burden of holding it all inside became agonizing, and I could no longer keep it confined. It yearned to be shared.

In my creative pursuits, I sometimes craft for the broader society—like cookbooks, perhaps, that sell like crazy and resonate with the masses.

And then there are moments when I create expressly for souls like mine, who share my thirst for truth and yearning for growth, who will appreciate my stream of consciousness and understand the depth of my thoughts.

This book in your hands is a piece of my soul reaching out to yours, a culmination of a decade's worth of relentless dedication and profound discoveries that have shaped my existence.

This is for all of you; I know you're out there.

Raizy

Contents

Introduction	1
Where I'm Coming From	13
Definition	27
The Anatomy of a Yenta	29
The First Step	39
The Ex-Yenta	45
From Gossip to Growth	55
Rise and Shine	63
Self-Esteem Essentials: A Practical Approach	83
Like a Lady	103
Tafkid & Talent	127
Friendships & Friend-Shifts	145
Nebach	173
Open Hearts, Open Minds	183
Who Do You Think You Are?	197
Shattered Reflections	205

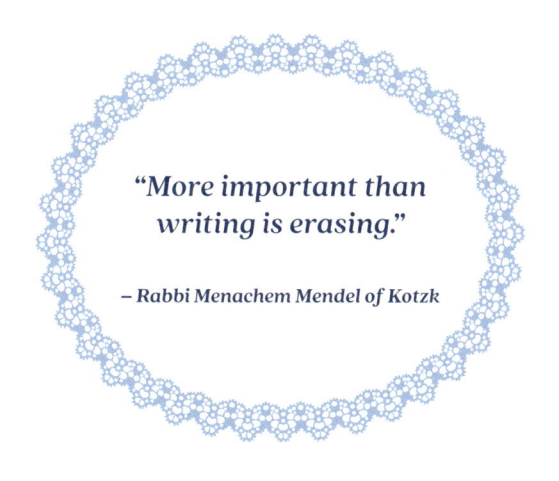

> "More important than
> writing is erasing."
>
> – Rabbi Menachem Mendel of Kotzk

INTRODUCTION

WHY I CAN'T WRITE THIS BOOK: A COMPILATION OF REASONS

2018

So here I am, sitting in front of my computer, typing the first chapter of my book at 12:43 AM on a Motza'ei Shabbos (02/11/2018). Just typing the words "my book" feels surreal. I mean, it's just a single Word file on my computer, and it's just a dream. Who says anyone will be interested in publishing my thoughts and stories? But you know what? I don't care. I'm doing this for me.

Let me backtrack a little. You see, I've always had this urge to write a book. There have been so many stories and struggles I've encountered that I felt I should write about. Yet, while I was swamped with countless ideas that would make an interesting book, every idea presented me with an issue.

First and foremost, writing a full-fledged autobiography would involve many details and aspects that don't only belong to me. If it were up to me, I would share a lot more than I already do, but I respect the people who respect me and wouldn't want to make them uncomfortable.

Then there's all the negativity. Too much negativity. The juicy stories, the events that shook me to the core and then sculpted me, include trauma, villains, hurt, and pain. So many parts I couldn't share, simply due to a breach of the laws of *lashon hara* (gossip or evil speech) or privacy.

At that point, my all-or-nothing personality kicked in. What's the point of writing a book about my life's journey when most of it is unshareable?

But then one Shabbos afternoon, as I was wistfully thinking about my goal to publish a book, a revolutionary thought crossed my mind. What if I could write my stories and encounters as an exercise? What if I could prove to the world that it's possible to relate a story effectively, without focusing on the villains and the negativity? What if I could write a book about the rosy results of life's challenges without getting down in the mud? What if I could write a book focused on the triumphs and lessons I've learned? On the insights I have to share?

You see, I never considered myself an optimist by nature. In general, I tend to protect and guard myself by keeping my hopes low, out of fear of being disappointed. But what if this book can be focused on accomplishments and how to get there, rather than my struggles?

That was it. With that, I decided to go all in for the challenge.

The fire was reignited. I felt increasingly excited. I saw myself with pen in hand ... until another layer of the dilemma was unveiled, revealing an angle I hadn't considered. There always seems to be another reason, another explanation for why this thing we desire so intensely is problematic. We, the ones eager to make it happen, are experts at conjuring up more excuses. The contemplation was far from over....

I thought about the type of book I wanted to write: a self-help memoir. I considered the non-Jewish books that feature women sharing their rawness, vulnerability, and speaking their minds. I love these books; they are often incredibly relatable, making me feel as if the author is speaking directly to me. And that's the kind of book I so wanted to create for our *oilem* (crowd) in our *shprach* (language).

But then I wondered—why *aren't* there more books about women sharing their musings, anecdotes, and thoughts in our Jewish market? That got me thinking. Was it because Jewish women are generally more modest? Would publishing a book about myself come off as immodest? Bragging? Yes, I even thought, "Who do you think you are?"

I pictured the bookshelves in the Judaica store, the popular *frum* female authors, and there was no denying that they mostly wrote fiction—oh, and cookbooks! Have we entered an era where self-expression is culturally unacceptable, or is it just a lack of confidence in the *heimishe* women of today?

These questions harassed me all Shabbos long. While I don't believe that sharing about yourself to entertain and inspire other women is inappropriate, the reality is that most women aren't doing it, and the related question, "Why aren't they doing it?" continued to plague me.

Then I thought about my journey on Instagram. How I was misunderstood by many at first, but with time, was understood and appreciated by most. It was exactly the same question. On the one hand, there weren't many other *heimishe* (especially *chassidishe*) women putting themselves out there when I started. At first, people didn't get what I was all about. To tell the truth, I didn't fully understand it either. But that's exactly what captured my audience—the fact that I just went for it, shared, and kept sharing fearlessly.

So, what if I do it again? What if I write a book about my journey, my struggles, and my musings? Who says only a cookbook or a novel is acceptable? What if I followed my gut and wrote whatever I felt compelled to share?

Who do I think I am?

Just a girl with a story.

I truly believe there is something to learn from everyone, and if my story can inspire or help just one person, then it will be worth it.

Motza'ei Shabbos had me at the computer. I had so many ideas! I sat and typed into the wee hours of the night. I labeled the document: "WHAT IF: ALL THE REASONS I CAN'T WRITE THIS BOOK." And I saved it on my computer.

After a few days, after writing another few pages, I took a step back to think and revisit my doubts. The files remained untouched until recently, when I mustered up the courage to revisit and rework them.

A year later, I decided to embark on a new writing project—a book about Shabbos. This felt like a safer topic to focus on. It was not about me. It was about highlighting the beauty of the Shabbos day, and included recipes.

2019
While working on my first book, *Lekoved Shabbos Kodesh,* I found myself writing a new chapter by accident. The words poured out of me. I wasn't assembling sentences but allowing my thoughts to emerge in a rushing stream.

At first, I experienced serenity and clarity, as I do every time I clearly express my emotions, opinions, and feelings in writing. But then I felt an overwhelming sense of anxiety and fear. Although I loved what I had written and felt compelled to share it with the world, I worried that others might misinterpret or twist my words, especially since it was a sensitive topic. I also feared this would end up being one of those decisions made in my young and stupid years, which I would later regret...

A knot in my stomach tightened with the prospect of unveiling personal truths to a public audience, and the unknown reactions and consequences.

It was on another Motza'ei Shabbos, around 3 AM, that I found myself in a state of confusion and turmoil. My husband and children were long lost in their dreams, and I had just finished an intense writing session. But instead of the usual post-writing bliss, a mix of exhaustion and exhilaration, I was just a mess. Instead of feeling accomplished, I felt torn and uncertain about what to do next.

Around that time, I had become friendly with Malky Weingarten, a brilliant scriptwriter and producer. I was drawn to Malky not only for her creativity and talent, but also for her kind heart and generosity. She was always full of life and positivity, and her home was always open to those in need.

In that moment of uncertainty, I immediately thought of Malky. She was older and wiser, and a creative writer. I knew she would understand.

I turned to Malky for advice. I sent her a long WhatsApp voice note, explaining my situation and asking for her guidance. I told her that I was writing a book about my creative journey, including chapters on my struggles in high school and my love for Shabbos. But while writing, something entirely different and unexpected came out. I found myself going off on a tangent and writing a whole chapter about some of the difficulties I've faced. I felt that it would be a captivating read, but I was afraid of exposing such a personal and painful part of my life to the world. I worried that it might ruin my children's chances for good schools or *shidduchim*, or make me appear socially off.

I was incredibly relieved to have another creative mind up with me in the wee hours of the night, along with a voice note in response just two minutes later. Malky is the queen of long voice notes. Malky's voice notes, like herself, are filled with *perel verter* (pearls of wisdom), as I would say in Yiddish. She gets right to the point, offers sage advice, and her humor always puts a smile on my face.

She made it clear that I was unusual. That I stood out. I wasn't the typical *chassidishe* woman, so I should forget about trying to fit into stereotypes, for that part was long gone. I was an Instagram star, I was driving, I was all over the place and different.

"You are not the typical *chassidishe* woman who cares about what everyone will say. Because if you did, you wouldn't be who you are now. You wouldn't be on Instagram doing what you do. You are confident in yourself. You know that what you are doing isn't just not wrong, it's right. It's right because you are using your talents to inspire and bring people closer to Hashem. You know that, and you know that really, really well."

She went on to tell me about her personal struggles in her younger years, her constant self-doubts and fears of the repercussions of her work, and the effects it might have on her children's future. But a huge weight was lifted off her shoulders when she came to realize that the right people not only won't be put off by what she did, they will love her for it. The right people loved that her house was always filled with happiness, for a happy, fulfilled mother who does what she loves makes a happy home.

"The right person, Raizy, will think that what you do is amazing! What you are saying about your life and growing up with questions—all of us had that. Questions make you a stronger, better person. I think it shows how *frum* and really solid you are now, because you are not just going through the motions. You have questioned, and you've found, and you've decided to be you, and you are so happy to be you! A truly smart person will appreciate that, not like those who are busy looking at the outside and worrying about what other people will say and think. A truly smart and *frum* person will appreciate that part of you and will consider it a plus. You need to be confident and strong here. I wish I could cut out those few uncertain years when I allowed people to make me feel like my personality was a problem."

I replied that she was right. I wasn't typical at all, I was out there and sharing. But this was different. It was very deep and personal. Yes, I showed my kitchen, pots, and office. From time to time, I exposed a little more. But this was entirely different. Writing all this in the right way, in the vulnerable way I wanted it to be written, would unveil my character and essence to the world.

"I know it's wonderful, and I don't need reassurance. I know it's beautiful, and that's why I want to write about it," I told Malky, "But still..."

As I expressed my hesitations to Malky, she listened attentively to my concerns. Despite my belief that sharing was beautiful, I questioned the wisdom of revealing a part of myself that most people wouldn't be comfortable sharing.

In truth, it was just fear—fear of rejection and being misunderstood.

Malky understood where I was coming from and offered her advice. She suggested that I put those chapters aside and save them for a time when I was more confident and ready to take that bold step. However, she also reminded me that I have plenty of other things to write about.

Her words were just what I needed to hear. I took the entire document and copied it into a new folder titled "Book #3." I went back to writing *Lekoved Shabbos Kodesh* with a sense of calm. It was a safe topic.

INTRODUCTION

2020

As the Lubavitcher Rebbe wisely said, "If you know *aleph*, teach *aleph*." I knew how to whip up a *heimishe* cholent and understood the essence of Shabbos, so I taught what I knew. I also understood Shabbos and the work required to create that special atmosphere, so I taught that too. Another thing I knew is that although I read *sefarim* (religious books), the average woman isn't buying a *sefer* on *oneg Shabbos*, but she will run to buy a cookbook with pretty pictures. So that's what I created. A book with recipes and pretty pictures, sprinkling in some extras I thought they could use. I packaged my passion with recipes. I embraced the lifestyle book concept.

Writing *Lekoved Shabbos Kodesh* was an incredible journey for me, and it's a project that still holds a very special place in my heart. The initial concept had been on my mind for a few years, but it wasn't until I realized that the book I wanted to read about Shabbos—a Shabbos lifestyle book—didn't exist, that I decided to create it myself. Shabbos is the central point of our lives, and I wanted to provide Jewish women with the tools and tips to bring that special Shabbos feeling into their homes.

As a *Yiddishe mamme* and homemaker, I know firsthand how challenging it can be to bring Shabbos into our homes, especially when we're exhausted at the end of the week. But I truly believe that it's a big part of our duties, and that we can all use as much empowerment and guidance as we can get. Both my husband and I grew up in true Hungarian *chassidishe* homes where Shabbos was glorified as it should be, so I felt I had the right background for this. I poured my heart and soul into this book, and it covers many elements of Shabbos. From the emotional mindset of how to enter Shabbos feeling like a queen, to practical ideas that include close to one hundred of my favorite recipes, along with hacks, table-setting ideas, flower care, and even Thursday night dinner ideas—this book has it all. It's more than a cookbook; it's a complete guide to living a Shabbos lifestyle.

Writing the book was an emotional experience. As I sat down to write, my home was filled with joy and a productive atmosphere that emanates from the creation of meaningful work. And as I wrote, I felt a deep sense of gratitude to the Ribono Shel Olam for giving me this opportunity.

The release of the first *Lekoved Shabbos Kodesh* book was an absolute triumph, *baruch Hashem* (thank G-d)! The momentum it gained exceeded all my expectations. Four years later, the feedback is still strong. The overwhelming success of the book has left me feeling humbled and grateful, with an indescribable sense of joy and pride in what I have accomplished.

One of the chapters that I kept getting feedback on was the chapter on entering Shabbos like a queen. I wrote about not being a martyr, and to instead be a *balabusta* with grace, knowing your true values and limits. I shared how I used to push myself, and what I learned over the years to help me establish a better balance. I was shocked by the overwhelming responses I received on that chapter. After all, everyone talks about self-care these days, right?

But then it hit me: while I had already reached my breaking point and helped myself, these women hadn't. They didn't have my experience; they hadn't read what I had through the years. They were just starting out on their journey, and my words were a breath of fresh air for them. That's when I realized how much was lacking, and it gave me the inspiration to keep going and give people what they truly needed.

2021
After seeing the positive response to the few chapters I included in the beginning of my Shabbos book, I felt compelled to write more. I had these files saved on my computer, these thoughts swirling around in my head, and this burning desire to share them with others. But I couldn't help wondering—would anyone take me seriously? It was a daunting thought, and I was afraid.

Eventually, I made the decision to wait until I was 35. In my mind, that was the age when people start taking you more seriously. For now, I decided to focus my attention on creating another cookbook. The first one did well. It was safe. And of course, I included a bit of inspiration at the beginning of the book, just as I did in the first one.

Writing my second book was a journey of channeling my creativity while keeping it safe. It was an insanely creative process that was both challenging and incredibly rewarding. I poured my heart and soul into every page, adorning each one with pastel hues, intricate details, and unique props sourced from all over the world. From styling and decorating to illustrating and spray-painting furniture, this project was an explosion of creativity and whimsy that I absolutely adored.

I was so excited to share the kid at heart part of myself with the world. The book was designed to be a heartwarming read for young and old alike, filled with sweet ideas and ways to enhance your Shabbos table, infusing every moment with sweetness, spirit, and love. Even though it was still on the theme of Shabbos, it had a completely different vibe compared to my first book. I expressed myself with every pastel hue, scallop, and whimsical dish.

2022
My second book, *Lekoved Shabbos Kodesh for Kids and Kids at Heart*, was also a great success, but after that, I knew I needed to move on. I felt a desire to express more than just the recipes in me.

As much as I enjoyed cooking and hosting, the food was never a goal in itself, but a means to an end. There was always a deeper meaning behind it all, and I sought a way to convey that. Shabbos served as the perfect example; it was the foundation, the subject of my first two books. Shabbos was the ideal starting point for my journey of self-expression, illustrating how food isn't materialistic when elevated with spiritual goals.

But I wanted more for us women. I craved to break the monotony of topics restricted to buses, ear infections, and gefilte fish recipes. It was time to broaden the conversation.

While I believe learning is important for every Jewish woman, I acknowledge that not everyone can engage in a *shiur* (Torah class). I knew we needed something down-to-earth and relatable, and I had the perfect vision. An online haven that would offer women a wellspring of inspiration and wisdom on every aspect of a Jewish woman's multi-dimensional life, presented with our special power of *hod*—beautiful and entertaining. Conversations and wisdom shared not in a preachy manner, but in our language, through captivating, woman-to-woman exchanges. I aimed to fill the void and create the uplifting and educational content I craved.

The Lubavitcher Rebbe wisely said, "When we look at the world and only see a problem, it's us who have the problem. But when we look at the world and see a solution, it means that this is the corner of the world we're meant to light up."

With a clear vision in mind, I set out to create a video platform that would offer education and inspiration on everything today's Jewish woman needs, from home decor and recipes to marriage and parenting advice. My passion for topics like motherhood, femininity, creativity, and relationships would take center stage, alongside practical kitchen tips—all neatly divided by category. A platform that would radiate with positive messages, support and empowerment for women.

My husband (my biggest supporter) and I embarked on the journey of building, filming, and curating this little haven for women, one step at a time. And before we knew it, we joyfully launched the video platform *Inspired Living*, along with its accompanying Raizy Fried app, and the reception was as warm and welcoming as ever.

2023

As they say in Yiddish, "*Der oilem iz arangekimmen klur*—the crowd came in loud and clear." The discussions I initiated on the video platform were resonating, and women were not only soaking them up but leaving rave reviews, expressing a thirst for more than just recipes.

The proof is in the pudding. As of today, *Inspired Living* boasts thousands of subscribers, and the feedback is off the charts. Women eagerly anticipate Tuesdays, when a new episode drops every week—it's become their special time to enjoy the episode and feel understood.

I feel humbled, privileged, and fortunate to be able to facilitate these life-changing conversations and deliver transformative content to women who appreciate it.

With a flourishing *Inspired Living* subscription base and a notebook brimming with ideas, topics, and guest suggestions lined up for the next seven years, it hit me. All this feedback was my cue. I recognized that if Hashem had orchestrated all this to happen through me, I could finally write my book.

It was about time!

INTRODUCTION

I began dusting off my old files from years back and adding new layers to them. My book was coming, in the right time, *b'sha'ah tovah*!

2024

Here it is. *The Book.*

A piece of my soul on these pages.

To my kindred spirits, this is crafted especially with you in mind! I see you. I feel you.

And to those who are not wired like me, for whom every struggle may not resonate, I sincerely pray that as you read, your heart and mind will open to the emotions and experiences within.

My concern extends beyond myself and my image; it extends to all those who share a similar journey. It's essential to open your mind to try to understand my experience, because you're bound to encounter another truth seeker at some point in your life, and it can be anyone—your sibling, your spouse, or your child. Learning to understand people like us will provide an opportunity for compassion towards another soul.

As you delve into these pages brimming with my experiences, reflections, and observations, my sincere wish is that only understanding and warmth unfold from my words. That our hearts harmonize with love and comprehension, to embrace our collective human experiences.

With warmth and love for the struggles of the soul searcher in this dark *galus*, and a deep yearning for the time when the world will be filled with the honor of Hashem and His eternal truth,

Raizy

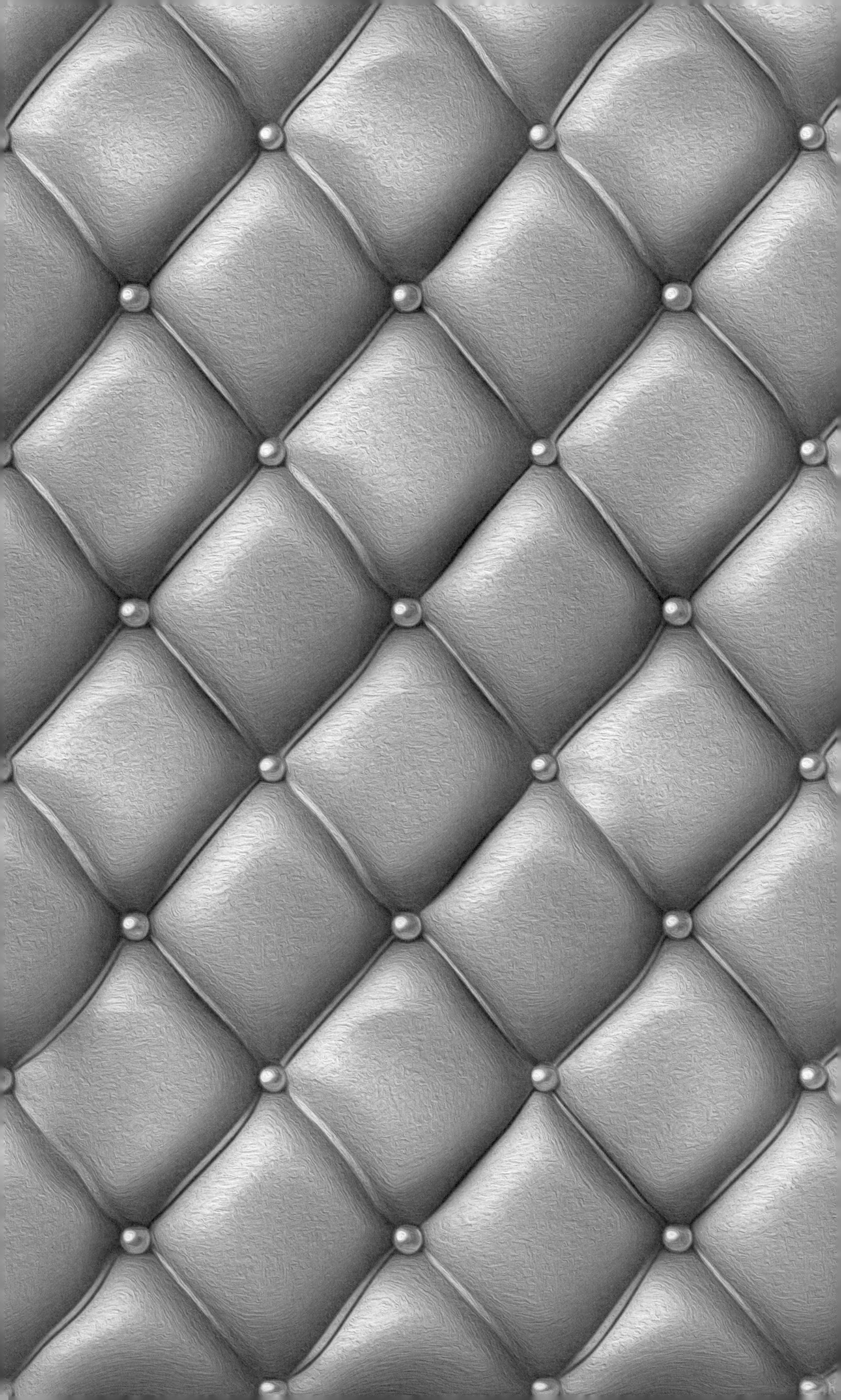

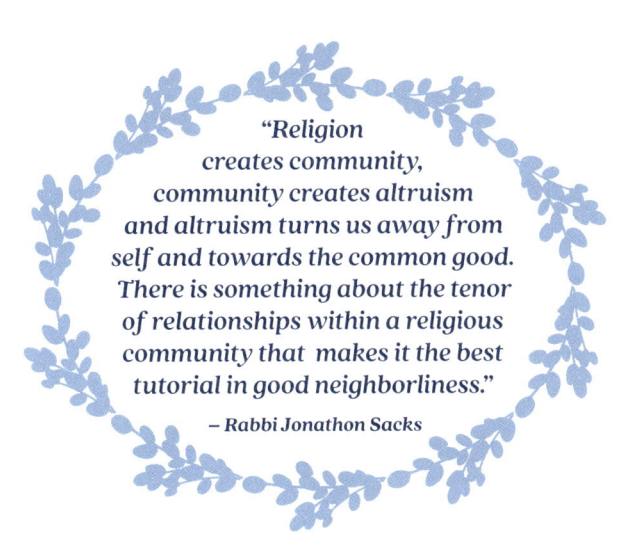

> "Religion creates community, community creates altruism and altruism turns us away from self and towards the common good. There is something about the tenor of relationships within a religious community that makes it the best tutorial in good neighborliness."
>
> – Rabbi Jonathon Sacks

WHERE I'M COMING FROM

IT'S EASY TO SPOT THOSE YOUNG COUPLES AS THEY stroll down the street. They announce themselves with their fashion choices, the tone of their social media posts, and the unconventional nature of their vacation plans. They express themselves by using brightly colored markers to color outside the lines that they've adhered to for so many years. This artistic rebellion extends beyond paper, as they experiment on their path to self-discovery.

This delayed teenage behavior is a prevalent occurrence in *chassidishe* circles, like mine, where children grow up in sheltered environments and often embark on the journey of marriage at a tender age.

It happens often. An average *chassidishe* boy marries a good, run-of-the-mill girl at the age of 19, and everything appears to be fine and dandy. However, as they step outside the sheltered walls of the system—leave their parents' home, their school, and yeshivah, and are exposed to the real world—they start to see things differently. They are immersed in a sea of exciting choices and begin challenging the status quo.

They are soon grappling with the blurred lines between what's right, what's normal, and what's extreme. The once-familiar boundaries have faded, leaving them both excited and bewildered by the uncharted territory that lies ahead. They get what the older generation would call "*feiglech in kup*, birds in their head"—toying with foreign beliefs or nonsense.

This young couple may find it a thrilling journey, but in this journey they face confusion, curiosity, and the gradual unraveling of their preconceived notions about life and societal norms. They are encountering a spectrum of perspectives that challenge their previously sheltered understanding.

The adventurous ones start testing the terrain and trying out new things. It's nerve-wracking for their parents who watch, shell-shocked, because they never expected their *voile* (well-behaved) children to be "that type." These kids had followed the rules religiously throughout elementary and high school, and suddenly, were acting out in ways their parents never saw coming.

Each young couple thinks they've discovered America when they uncover the flaws in the system, feeling remarkably enlightened and convinced that only they can see it. They walk around feeling exceptionally clever, certain that the older generation is blindly following the rules. In their quest to resist being mere followers, they may step out of line excessively, lacking a clear understanding of where to draw boundaries, as the Yiddish saying goes, "*Zei veisen nisht vee an, vee ois*—they don't know where to draw the line."

As children, we eat what we are fed, and we tend to accept what we're taught without question. It's only as we grow older, develop critical thinking skills, and begin to explore the world around us that we start to question what we've been taught. Not everyone takes it to the same extremes. Not everyone is a soul searcher or boundary pusher. Many people are perfectly content with what the system has taught them all through life, and that's a beautiful thing. It's called *temimus*—innocent faith.

The thing with *temimus* is, you can't fake it. You need to be born with it.

For the soul searchers who are trying to discover their identities, the later it happens, the more challenging it gets. Because if you only embark on the messy journey after you're married, it's not just you: there's a spouse in the picture now. Sometimes it works out beautifully, as they both navigate the world together and find their place. But it can also cause a lot of tension!

While the world views such behavior as typical teenage rebellion, the complexity intensifies for these couples. Having been sheltered all their lives and married extremely young, all this experimenting is often happening when couples already have one or two children. There are *mosdos* involved, and there's so much at stake. It's much more complex to go through the process of finding your identity when you're already expected to be a responsible adult making responsible decisions.

I am grateful to have gone through my teenage self-discovery phase as a real teenager, in high school. I grew up in a traditional *chassidishe* household, surrounded by old-school beliefs and a strong sense of *chassidishe* pride. I was content and happy in my upbringing. However, things started to shift as I entered my teenage years and experienced the full force of adolescence. I didn't enjoy school, and struggled to fit in with my typical-minded classmates who thought more conventionally.

I'll be the first to admit that I wasn't the easiest child for my parents to deal with. However, by the time I turned 18 and began looking for a *shidduch* (marriage partner), I was ready and eager to get married, and my parents knew exactly what to look for in a potential match. I was fortunate to find a boy who was on the same page as I was, and there were no unpleasant surprises down the line. Everything happened faster for me, which wasn't easy—but today I'm so grateful.

Many people carry their emotional baggage for years. This emotional weight causes them to suffer from back pain, anxiety, panic attacks, and other issues for a big part of their lives. I consider myself fortunate to have crashed and gotten the wake-up call when I was 24, which forced me to confront the traumas I've been through. It was hard work, but it allowed me to do the emotional labor that many people don't get to until much later in life.

I share all of this so you can truly grasp where I'm coming from as you delve into the pages of this book.

Though my youth may imply naivete, I have been enriched with experiences that have granted me a distinct outlook on the world. I have witnessed the system's frailties, and I have fearlessly explored alternative ideas and ideologies.

As a speaker and writer for the public, one of the valuable lessons I've learned on the job is to navigate the delicate balance of expressing my views without alienating those who may not share them. It's important to work *bein hatipot*, between the drops, because I understand that everyone may not be on the same wavelength as I am.

Unfortunately, many people tend to be very black and white in their thinking, quick to judge and marginalize those who stray from the norm and adjust the beat to their own drum. As a result, I must be mindful of the way I express myself when sharing my thoughts with the world. I will never pretend to be something I'm not, but I must always bear in mind the responsibility I have to my family and my children's future. While I value vulnerability and authenticity, I also strive to maintain a certain level of class and dignity.

It's unfortunate that some people feel threatened by women who speak their minds and challenge conventional thinking. This marginalization is something that I've experienced continuously over the years, and it has left me feeling deeply misunderstood.

I vividly recall one instance early in my married life, when I was engaged in deep conversation with seemingly like-minded women at a wedding. It was one of those conversations that discuss the flaws of "the system." Together we were bemoaning the things that don't make sense, the things that are unfair, and so on.

It was a good conversation and it felt like we were all on the same page, until one of the women turned to me and asked, "*Nu*, so when are you taking off your band?" She was referring to the headband I wear on top of my wig, which is a traditional chassidic garb. And that's when I realized: we were not on the same page at all. Once again, I was misunderstood. I'll never forget the sinking feeling that washed over me. In a single moment, the warmth of camaraderie was replaced with a sense of isolation—and a sense of how foolish I was for assuming that these women understood me.

I have always cherished *chassidishe* customs, particularly those that align with my personal values. I wear the band that adorns my wig with pride. Must I abandon all of my traditions simply because I have identified some flaws in the system? Just dump it all—the baby with the bathwater?

A more recent example that struck a painful chord in my heart was when I received a phone call after the publication of my first book, *Lekoved Shabbos Kodesh*. The caller introduced herself as one of the editors on the board of a magazine I used to write for.

"Raizy!" she exclaimed. "Yesterday, I walked into my local Judaica store and saw this beautiful new Shabbos book. As I was skimming through the pages with these stunning Shabbos pictures and writing that expresses the beauty and pride of our *heilige* (holy) Shabbos, I thought to myself that the woman who created this book must be someone really solid, who gets it. Then I checked the cover of the book and saw that it says Raizy Fried. I was so surprised because I remember you from when you worked here. You know, you were so out of the box, and this book is so in the box!"

I cannot recall how I responded or how I ended the conversation, but what I'll always remember is that painful pit in my stomach. Ouch—how that hurt! It cut me deeply, and I had a hard time calming down.

My husband did not understand why I was so upset. "Take it as a compliment," he said. "She didn't mean to be hurtful."

While I knew he was right and that the caller had good intentions of complimenting my work, her comment hit a nerve—a raw and vulnerable one, created through years of feeling misunderstood and undervalued. Despite my best efforts to communicate effectively and express myself clearly, there were always some who failed to grasp the essence of who I am and what I stood for. It seemed like no matter what I did, no matter how hard I tried, certain people would always be unable to understand or appreciate me.

That editor couldn't fathom how an open-minded person like me could create a traditional, spiritual Shabbos book. She failed to realize that it's precisely because I'm open-minded that I'm able to deeply appreciate and value the meaningful traditions that make Shabbos so special.

Here's the thing: being open-minded doesn't mean that you lack conviction or that you're easily swayed by every passing idea. On the contrary, being open-minded means that you're willing to entertain different viewpoints while remaining rooted in your core beliefs. It means being able to look beyond the surface and see the deeper meaning. To create something solid, something that truly resonates with people, you must be solid in your beliefs. And that solidity often comes after wrestling with the truth, from questioning, from seeking.

Creating something truly meaningful requires a deep connection to one's beliefs and values, not blind adherence to old ideas. I've always been one to question things, to seek out the deeper meaning behind everything. This quest isn't a wishy-washy state of being. It's precisely because of that search that I've been able to find such beauty and depth in the traditions and customs of *Yiddishkeit* (Judaism).

In my past writing, I have touched on the theme of being misunderstood and my difficult experiences in school. The preface, introduction, and "Soul Searching for Shabbos" chapter in my second book, *Lekoved Shabbos Kodesh for Kids & Kids at Heart*, was dedicated to help the children who, like me, struggle in school. But what I shared was just a small part of my story. While I have received praise for my vulnerability, I have only scratched the surface.

I was bullied way beyond my high school years. Calls from high school teachers and my principal intruded upon the innocent cocoon of our first furnished apartment, shattering its coziness and my peace. They relentlessly disturbed me during the blissful period of my *shanah rishonah* (first year of marriage).

If you've read my other books, you know how much I despised school. High school seemed endless; I felt like I was confined in jail. When I was finally released, got married, and began to live happily with my husband, they came after me.

It felt like everything was too good to be true, like I was trapped in a web I could never escape.

My early twenties were a time of seething pain, heartbreak, and soul suffering. I was bullied relentlessly and tormented by people who wanted to tear down my essence. They shattered my confidence and peaceful existence. It took a lot of time and effort to find my inner peace and establish myself again.

I've been called many things. As a young teenager in school, it was *apikores*. At 24, when it all came crashing down, I was called *chazer fleish* (pig meat) in front of my husband, simply for not fitting a mold that people desperately wanted me squashed into. When I heard Rabbi Wallerstein *zt"l* share his experience of being called a "sewer rat" in yeshivah, I started bawling.

The dam had burst, and that was just the beginning.

Over the years, being fortunate to have the confidence to fearlessly foster connections with many great individuals, I have had the privilege of speaking with numerous respected *rabbanim* (rabbis). They have all privately shared similar stories with me. They, too, were misunderstood growing up, and today they are Torah giants and leaders. My whole view is different now. I understand that what I went through is simply a part of the process.

I have many juicy stories, but I chose not to go into them. Aside for *lashon hara*, I do not want to be perceived as someone who is bashing the system. While I used to envy those who chose to speak their minds freely, I now realize that it's also about maturity and foresight.

I shared all of this for a reason. It's come to this:

While it's true that the system can stifle individuality, I have come to recognize that societal structures serve an important purpose in upholding values and traditions. Without these structures, it can be easy to lose sight of what's truly important and become lost in the chaos of modern life. Role models are essential to inspire and propel us forward on our path.

I've seen the damage that can occur when we abandon these structures altogether and let modern individualism rule our lives. Today, many of our generation's *oifgeklerte*, the "enlightened" and progressive individuals who have dared to step out of the box, are losing touch with the essence of Judaism and traditional wisdom by embracing progressive ideology, which unfortunately lacks the truth and substance that our souls need to flourish. It's disheartening to see a growing influx of secular-left-progressive-woke ideology infiltrating our *frum* culture, particularly among our confused, impressionable young people.

More and more, our Torah values and traditional wisdom are being cast aside, as woke individualism takes hold. "Who I am" becomes ruled by emotions, feelings, and desires over reason. This is the abandonment of reason itself.

These are not necessarily rebellious individuals. Anyone might be drawn to a way of life that labels itself as kind and accepting and prioritizes equality, especially if they have faced challenges, trauma, or been exposed to the negative side of the old ways. I have been down that road myself, and I understand the appeal of this ideology.

However, the problem with much of pop psychology and progressive ideology is that first, much of it doesn't align with our Torah values. Today's pop psychology often perpetuates an unempowered life of excuses and victim mentality. This is similar to Freud's etiology, which focuses on cause and effect and can lead to determinism, which brings about feelings of helplessness and resignation.

In contrast, the psychology of teleology, created by Austrian psychiatrist Alfred Adler, promotes the idea that individuals have agency and can make choices that lead to positive outcomes, regardless of past trauma or setbacks. Adler believed that individuals have the power to shape their own destiny through lifestyle choices. He rejected the notion of determinism and instead championed the idea of courage, which involves overcoming obstacles to achieve one's goals. According to Adler, "It's not what one is born with but what use one makes of the equipment." This approach recognizes that everyone has unique strengths and weaknesses; it's how we use these traits that ultimately defines our success.

Adler's perspective is aligned with Torah values and the concept of *avodas hamiddos* (improving our character traits), as it promotes personal responsibility and encourages individuals to take charge of their lives, using their talents and abilities to create a positive future. Unfortunately, Adler's approach is not in accordance with today's pop psychology trends.

Another issue with these beliefs is that they function almost like a religion in the lives of many of our *frum* millennials. While they come from Torah-observant homes, they have never taken the time to explore the real Torah beyond the elementary version of Noach and the *teivah* (ark), the do's and don'ts. Sadly, pop psychology is the only religion they have ever really known.

These young adults have been exposed to a simpler way, one that seems easier to understand and adopt. They have moved on to what they perceive as greater and better things. They have developed a certain intellectual elitism and view the previous generation with a critical eye, considering themselves more advanced and emotionally attuned than they really are. They consider themselves well-educated—and in some ways they are, but only in their chosen field. They feel that they are advancing social justice by promoting values they believe to be right and virtuous.

They have disregarded our Torah way and have never given it another glance or chance. While they may be well-educated in progressive ideology and other areas, they are often ignorant when it comes to the basics of Torah values, for they have never taken the time to educate themselves in our solid, ancient wisdom. Consequently, they are often unhappy and blame their upbringing, the system, and everything but woke ideology.

We live in an era of openness. The internet has brought about many benefits, but it also presents a challenge. It's a platform that allows for the dissemination of beliefs that do not align with the truth—especially our truth. Those who have left our *derech* (path) often take it upon themselves to make the world a better place by speaking out on various platforms and shows. They may be well-educated and articulate, but their eloquence can deceive viewers into believing they have a profound understanding of Jewish education. However, they often lack the basic knowledge of the basis of their claims, and their messages are filled with misinformation.

A common situation I have come across is OTD feminists who speak about their childhood "cult lives" and misconstrue the blessing of *shelo asani isha* as oppression. It is actually empowering when understood in context.[1]

When I come across these videos, I am not worried about the outside world hearing these things. I am worried about our own, the young people within our community who are listening and nodding along with these messages, buying into the misinformation and lies about their own religion. Many of these individuals are hurt and are struggling, and they may not have a firm grasp on the truth. It's these young people who we need to reach out to and educate, to provide them with the knowledge and tools to navigate the challenges they face and help them find their way back to the Truth. My heart aches for the future generation that is being initiated into a way of life that often contradicts the ways of the Torah.

It is not just those who have completely left religion that I worry about, but also those within our communities who are being influenced by ideas that are slowly making themselves comfortable in places where they don't belong. As a society, we are inundated with progressive ideas that sound beautiful and well-meaning, but don't always align with the ways of the Torah. We have leaders in the world of marriage and parenting who lead from a purely progressive mentality, advocating for a style of *chinuch* (education) that lacks basic rules of *derech eretz* (behaving respectfully) that are essential for children to become respectable and functioning adults.

Certain parenting classes are taught by educators who are coming from an inner-child place and leading with the heart of their childhood. Their inner child is still rebelling against the discipline they didn't like growing up, the authority they didn't want to follow. Now their agenda and focus is on respecting children. And while children should

---

[1] I recommend the book *Thank You G-d for Making Me A Woman* by Rabbi Aaron L. Raskin for more information on this topic.

be treated properly and with empathy, and while compassion is an important Torah value, there are also rules that a child must abide by. Parents need to be respected. There's a reason we are given children as adults—because a sane world needs adults raising children, not children raising children. Responsible parents need to set a fundamental foundation for a healthy life.

As someone who has been down that route, read all those books, taken those classes and bought into it all, I can empathize with those who are still caught in that mindset. We are living in a generation where we are taking in too many of these secular humanistic values. Thankfully, I caught myself in time to change and embrace the wisdom of the Torah. Even secular conservatives recognize that "being nice" lacks substance when it's void of ancient truths and core biblical wisdom.

Yet, despite the many challenges we face in this gray *galus* (exile), I remain hopeful. I hope that by sharing my stories and the lessons I have learned, I can inspire others to also become determined truth seekers, to seek out the light hidden in the darkness and confusion. We may not be able to fix the world, but we can take responsibility for our own growth and development. We can strive to become better versions of ourselves, to learn and grow through our ancient traditions and Torah wisdom.

My voice may exude youthfulness and spiritedness, but it is also infused with the wisdom and maturity that comes from facing life's harsh realities head-on. I have been trapped in the darkness and emerged with a deeper understanding and appreciation of our deep-rooted truths. I have traveled a path that led me from liberalism to conservatism, and speak from a place of conviction and passion. It is from this place that I share my insights with you—that's where I'm coming from!

In this book I'll share some of my personal journey of transformation, as I moved away from embodying the stereotypical yenta persona and towards a more mature and refined version of myself. From a moody, argumentative young woman to someone who rations her energy for the use of good and values the importance of inner peace and genuine connection with others.

In this book I'll share how I learned to shift my perspective and went from being an *oif-geklerte* (smarter than) millennial, to appreciating and rallying for the old-school wisdom.

I invite you to come along with me on this journey of ongoing self-growth and transformation. Let's learn how to look at things differently together! Let's learn how to be the kind of women who inspire and uplift others, who radiate love and light wherever we go. Let's be the kind of women our *bubbes* and *zeides* would be proud of, while still adding our own millennial flair.

Snuggle up with your favorite blanket, make yourself comfortable, and let's get down to business, ladies!

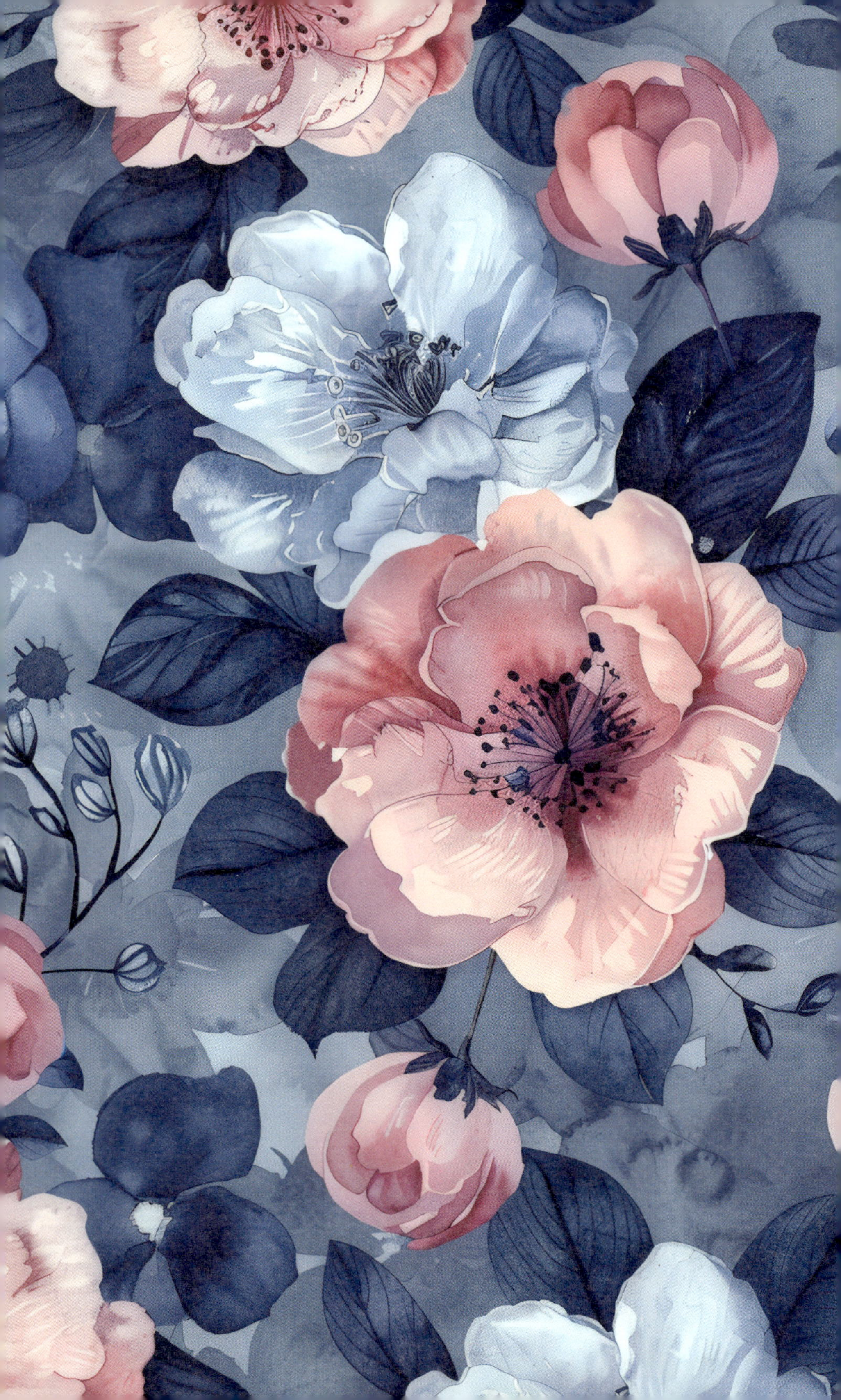

DEFINITION

yenta

[yen-t*uh*]

Phonetic (Standard) IPA

noun
Slang.
  1. a person, especially a woman: one that meddles

    also : BLABBERMOUTH, GOSSIP

Example of *yenta* in a sentence:

The couple's loud quarrel had the building's *yentas* yapping for a week.

Raizy's *Peirush* (Commentary)

What is a yenta?

A yenta isn't merely someone who constantly pokes her nose into others' affairs. A yenta is someone who talks endlessly about others, someone who thrives on drama.

There's definitely a yenta spectrum. On one extreme, there are women with big eyes and loud mouths whose lives revolve around other people's news and drama. They are addicted, restless, and tactless, bombarding you with nosy questions. On the opposite end, there are those dressed in pearls who gossip discreetly in a seemingly classy fashion. In reality, a "Classy Yenta" is an oxymoron, because making other people's lives your business is the complete opposite of classy!

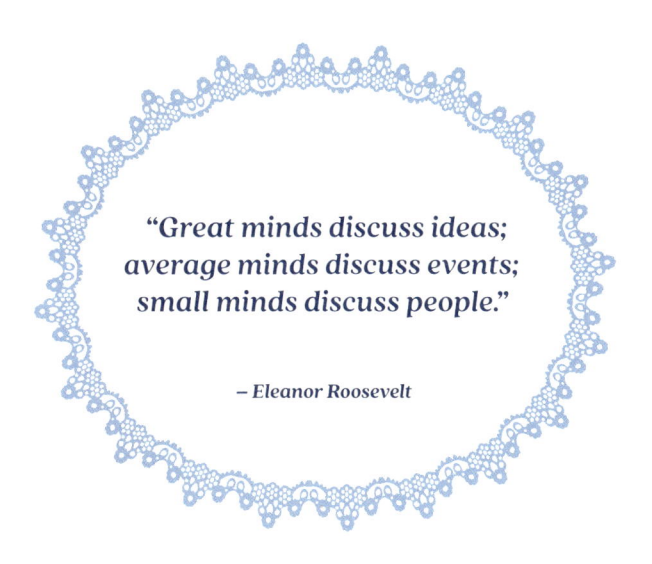

> "Great minds discuss ideas;
> average minds discuss events;
> small minds discuss people."
>
> – Eleanor Roosevelt

THE ANATOMY OF A YENTA

WHENEVER THAT AUNT WALKED IN ON OUR gatherings for *shalosh seudos* (the last meal eaten on Shabbos), my heart would sink, and I would think, "Here we go again." We were always in the middle of a juicy and thrilling conversation. And then she would appear, like a dark cloud on the horizon.

In Yiddish, we have an expression, "*S'iz meer shvartz gevuren far dee oigen*, I saw black before my eyes," and that's exactly how I felt. Those animated conversations were the lifeblood of our gatherings, the moments when we felt most alive. But when this aunt arrived, everything changed. She managed to suck all the joy out of the room.

As a teenager, I relished the heat of discussions, savoring the thrill of a good argument until I was practically blue in the face. And of course, I couldn't get enough of the latest updates on people and juicy gossip. But whenever that aunt was around, the mood would shift, and dread would fill me. It seemed like she had an issue with every topic we broached. Even if we didn't talk negatively about others, even if it didn't fall under the category of *lashon hara*, she would clamp down on the conversation. Whenever we were discussing *vus tit zeech bei yenem*, what was happening in other people's homes, she quickly put an end to it with the classic reminder about the importance of privacy: "*Ma tovu ohalecha Yaakov.*"

When we spoke about ourselves and our own pesky, unwanted hair, discussing the merits of waxing versus other hair removal methods, our aunt's disapproving glare was enough to make us stop in our tracks. She would make us feel like we were discussing something scandalous. Our aunt's stern, darting eyes could make a hardened criminal feel guilty, let alone a bunch of teenage girls and women just trying to look presentable.

For some reason, any conversation about basic grooming challenges was inappropriate around her young girls, even if we were just trying to tame our unibrows. It was infuriating. I would roll my eyes in exasperation. I remember thinking, "What on earth were we supposed to talk about if every topic is problematic?"

Was everything *lashon hara*, not *tzniusdig* (modest), or inappropriate? Were we only supposed to talk about the riveting topics of nature, or the benevolence of the Almighty?

Although I still cannot fathom why my aunt was so paranoid about her young girls hearing about the concept of grooming eyebrows, I am ashamed of the person I used to be. I distinctly remember feeling empty, like there was nothing else captivating in the world if we couldn't discuss people. Nowadays, I actually find ongoing conversations about people tiresome.

Make no mistake. My reasons for steering clear of discussing people are far from altruistic. It's just that I am now drawn to real topics that intrigue me, ones that allow me to delve deeper into emotions and other complex concepts. I enjoy conversations that uplift me and make me feel good about myself. Don't get me wrong—I am not an angel. Every once in a while, I'll indulge in a juicy scoop. I am only human, after all. But I do not dwell in the drama like I once did. It is no longer my sole interest, nor does it provide me with the sustenance that it once did.

I didn't make a conscious decision that "I'm going to stop speaking *lashon hara!*" That would have been futile. I believe it was a byproduct of my overall self-improvement journey, as I confronted my inner turmoil and worked through my negative emotions. As I delved deeper into my own soul, seeking to understand and heal the wounds within, I found myself becoming more attuned to the inner workings of others, rather than focusing on their external qualities.

Something changed when I started cleaning up my being, cleaning away the dirt and the hurt to unveil my essence and get in touch with my soul. It changed when I polished up my self-esteem, when I started establishing myself, sharpening my maturity and deciding where I wanted to use my energy. Slowly, as my mindset changed, my interests changed.

It's similar to when you're expecting a baby and suddenly you start noticing strollers everywhere you go. Or when you're shopping for a new coat, and all you can see are coats. When you're doing the inner work, or rather, as I like to call it in our *shprach* (language)—when you start working on your *middos* (character traits), it becomes the primary focus of your mind. You become so consumed with feeling your emotions and not running away from yourself that it can become overwhelming at times, like starting a new diet and obsessing over what you can eat for the first few weeks. But over time, these new habits become ingrained in you, and you naturally find yourself more interested in discussing deeper concepts, rather than empty gossip.

So one nice day I found myself in a circle where women were dissecting people, moving on from one person to the next—and I was horrified. I realized that my interests have changed. And I don't even know how. It's because I have changed.

It sounds all nice and dandy here, but I'll tell you from experience that when that realization hit, I didn't feel so good at all. I didn't feel holy or good about myself. It was kind of depressing when I realized I had outgrown my old ways of interacting with people. Suddenly, everyone seemed shallow and unenlightened, and I struggled to connect with my old friends who were still caught up in these conversations. My friends weren't necessarily interested in discussing limiting beliefs and how to overcome them, just because that was my thing. I felt stuck in a room full of shallow gossip when all I wanted was to have a deep and meaningful conversation.

I felt alone.

The hardest part of this journey was undoubtedly the loss of camaraderie. As I grew and evolved, I found myself drifting apart from those who couldn't meet me where I was. It was painful to let go of relationships that were once so important, but I came to realize that some friendships are not meant to last forever. Instead, I had to seek out new connections with people who shared my interests and could help me continue to grow.

I have a strong belief and theory when it comes to the topic of yentas and gossip. I firmly believe that when women stop learning, they stop growing. When they become complacent and only focus on getting through the day, when life revolves around gossiping in the park or on the phone to push the time until 6:30, when they can finally start bath time for their little ones... they are not thriving, they are barely surviving.

When I hear a woman constantly complaining about her mother-in-law, neighbor, or the bus driver, I feel bad for her. I know that the problem is not usually the people she's complaining and gossiping about; it's often a sign that she's stuck in a rut. She's not learning, growing, or creating. She's full of untapped potential and energy that needs to be channeled in a constructive, healthy way.

When women thrive on gossip and drama, it's usually because they are missing fulfillment or excitement in their lives.

"Oh my! You heard she's getting divorced?"

"Say *wwhaaaat?!?!*"

Now, there's some excitement! Something to discuss! Something to talk about!

Discussing someone else's divorce may be thrilling, but it's not a meaningful way to connect with others. It's a sad, empty life.

Also remember this:
Those who talk to you about others, talk to others about you.

Read that again.

When you choose to surround yourself with those *geshmake* people who deliver piping hot scoops to your door, remember that they make other deliveries, too.

And if you're the one who people are clamoring around with open mouths... Know that while they inch closer to listen, they also have zero respect for you, because they see what you're all about. They know the truth of life: *Those who talk to you about others, talk to others about you.*

I believe that the battle against *lashon hara* is a lost one when women are out of touch with themselves and their interests, and have nothing else to talk about besides taking apart other people. It's important for women to discover themselves and cultivate their passions, to explore their curiosity, to find meaningful topics to delve into. When women start learning and filling up their brains with new ideas, they naturally start speaking differently.

When women realize that they deserve better, and learn how much better life can be—things change automatically. Women need to start striving for genuine and meaningful relationships, rather than surface-level entertainment based on gossip. Every woman deserves to experience the uplifting feeling of genuine connection.

I believe that rather than simply banning gossip and negative speech, it's important to teach women how to be *more*. How to form meaningful social connections and have conversations that enrich their lives. By replacing the need for juicy gossip with exciting discussions about personal growth, shared interests, and creative pursuits, we foster a culture of growth and positivity. This shift leads to a more fulfilling life and deeper connections with others.

Whenever I get fired up about a topic, I tend to share my thoughts with my friends. And as I passionately shared my strong opinions on this topic with my friends, I was met with different perspectives and opinions.

One of my friends claimed that being a yenta is an inherent trait and that such people will never change. "I know those people, it's a type," she said. However, I disagree that being a yenta and personal growth are mutually exclusive. I believe we are all capable of much more than just gossiping and meddling in others' affairs. We are all on this earth to work on our character traits and create a meaningful life for ourselves.

Another friend suggested that knowing everyone and everything isn't necessarily bad. It can be used for good. Become a *shadchan* (matchmaker), she said. And she's got a point. There's nothing wrong with being well-connected and using those connections for good.

But it's not just about staying busy or using our connections for good. We must find true fulfillment and purpose in our lives.

One friend said it's not just about staying busy. "We're doing fine in the busy department!" she said. So many women have 9-to-5 jobs. It's not about filling the hours in your day, but about being truly fulfilled. "Who you are is not necessarily what you do," she said. It's about developing your identity.

Hint—your identity is not being a mother, or your profession.

These conversations fueled my passion and curiosity. The more I dug into the topic, the more I realized how broad and multifaceted it was. There were so many angles to explore, from the root of the problem of what makes a yenta a yenta, to traits ranging from curiosity to the need to be seen, and how one can evolve. I discovered a plethora of ideas and points to explore, such as curiosity, self-esteem, and how to desire more from life.

A related topic that emerged was empathy. Many yentas lack basic empathy skills; they sit and discuss everyone without knowing the *aleph beis* of being empathetic. They bombard you with questions or pity stares, completely missing the mark. Tact! Social etiquette, I realized, is a topic that you could literally write a book about (insert winky emoji here). One thing I knew for certain is that I would continue to explore this topic.

You see, when there's a problem, I'm a very big proponent of getting to the core, and not getting distracted by the superficial and blinding side effects.

For example: A couple sitting in a restaurant, both on their phones, can be a frustrating sight. Many people blame smartphones. I believe it goes deeper. Planning a date night takes a lot of effort and time. I don't believe that a woman scouts for a babysitter, gets all dressed up, and goes through all that effort just to eat an overpriced meal while fixating on her phone. I believe there's a deeper issue at play, such as hurt, difficulty being present, or running away from something. Let's not blame the phones for a lack of connection. This same couple in the restaurant twenty years ago would probably be reading newspapers, fighting, or just staring into space, bored stiff.

When it comes to gossip, I believe one of the core issues with yentas is not a lack of knowledge regarding the harsh effects of *lashon hara*. It's also not just a matter of self-control. I think a significant cause can be their lack of interest in anything else—no sense of purpose in life, no mission, and no spiritual connection. To step out of the yenta zone and create a rich, fulfilling life, we must first discover who we are.

For many women, the biggest problem is not that they don't dream big, but that they don't dream at all. It's the dead zone of buried dreams and potential that not only suffocates the dignity of those they discuss, but theirs as well.

So much of the "don't speak *lashon hara*" mantra we grew up with was outwardly focused. What many fail to realize is that every time we are negative about someone else, that energy affects us, too. Every time we judge someone else, it's a projection of our own selves. When we criticize another, we are actually highlighting the parts of ourselves that we don't accept or haven't been given permission to express. It's like the well-known saying: when you point your finger at another, there are three fingers pointing back at *you*.

Whatever you focus on in life, you tend to attract more of it. If I'm gossiping about someone I'm judging or criticizing, I'm actually fostering more negativity inside myself and diverting my focus from what I truly want.

To be a successful woman, it's crucial to stay focused on what *you* want to produce in life. What are your goals? What qualities do you want to experience?

If you're expending energy on other people's issues or drama, then you won't progress toward your goals or reach your full potential.

This book is essentially about stopping the gossip, but it's not just another discussion of the negative impacts of *lashon hara*. You won't find any trite analogies about feathers in the wind here. Instead, we will explore the harm that gossiping can cause not to others, but to yourself, and what you miss out on when you thrive on the sugar rush of the juice. We'll examine how this behavior often leaves you feeling parched and unfulfilled, always searching for that next hit of gossip to quench an insatiable thirst.

The focus of this book is on evolving and finding true fulfillment in life, not just in cheap thrills. Gossip may offer a temporary rush, but it ultimately fails to bring us any meaningful satisfaction.

At the end of the day, we are all so much more than yentas and meddlers. It's time to fill that void, to graduate and evolve. To tune into our purpose and build a lifestyle we can truly be proud of.

I want each one of you to explore your curiosity so you can enjoy discussing your visions and ideas.

I want you to build authentic connections with real friends.

I want you to attract women who inch closer to you, not for sensational stories, but for *you*.

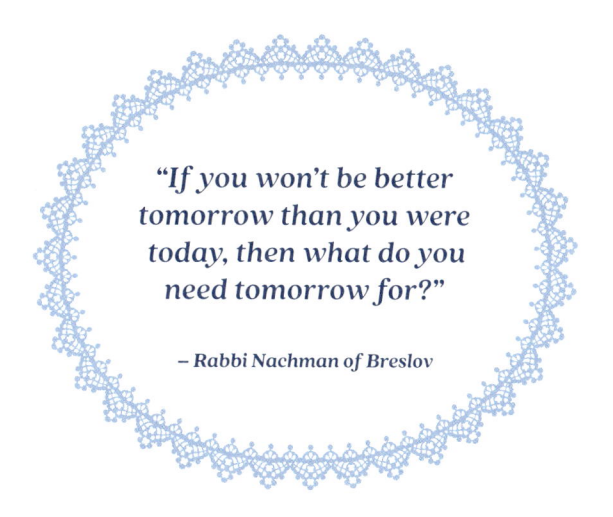

> *"If you won't be better tomorrow than you were today, then what do you need tomorrow for?"*
>
> – Rabbi Nachman of Breslov

THE FIRST STEP

THERE ARE THINGS THAT PEOPLE ASK ME ALL THE time, like how to become more confident. And I don't have any advice to share. I really don't. I was born this way. Ever since I can remember, I was always confident. I couldn't understand how or why people were not.

I remember back in elementary school when we all had Lands' End Trapper Keepers that had a lifetime guarantee. Remember Trappers? Remember the Lands' End Trappers that came with matching long, cylinder-shaped pencil cases in a variety of solid colors, each with a different colored zipper? Remember the guarantee and how we switched them out every year or even sooner for a new one in a different color?

I don't recall if Lands' End had a five-year guarantee or a lifetime guarantee for their products, but what I do remember is being on the phone with them all the time. You see, my mother isn't the type to *mach zeech meshuga* (make herself crazy) with these things, but I wanted a new sweater or a different color Trapper. So I called them, described the wear and tear, went to the tiny mailing store on

44th Street off 13th Avenue, shipped mine back, and got a fresh new one. Everyone and their neighbors were doing it.

Then there were those who desired to do the same, but were unsure. "I don't know how."

"What do you mean? You just call them and explain that your fabric got faded or whatever."

"But I don't know what to say."

"I'm embarrassed to call."

"I can't do these official calls."

"It's not my type."

I remember thinking, "Seriously? Who are they worried about? This anonymous lady sitting on the other end of the line in Wisconsin?"

Even if you stutter and make mistakes, who cares? She doesn't know you. She doesn't see you. She doesn't care about you; she's just doing her job.

I couldn't understand what their problem was, but I also felt sorry that they were missing out on the thrill of having a fresh new Trapper every few months, so I offered my services. I would call for them. I sat on the phone with Lands' End all day, not because I had so many things to exchange, but because I was the intermediary, the *shliach tzibbur*. I loved manipulating my voice to sound professional and secretarial. I loved updating my friends about my transactional accomplishments.

Don't sue me, it was 100% legal. Oh, the things I did. I should probably stop here.

The things I write about and share are lessons I've learned and challenges I've overcome through my own experiences. I never attended school for cooking, decorating, or public speaking; I simply enjoy sharing what I've discovered. Whether it's how to make fluffier challos, an easy hack to lift long salmon slices from a pan without it breaking (use an offset spatula like the OXO Good Grips Bent Icing Spatula, 12.75 inches long), or a mindset shift that brings more peace into life, I find joy in passing on these insights.

My innate urge to share is something I've felt since birth—it's a core part of who I am. This sharing personality is driven by a deep-seated desire to enrich others' lives with practical wisdom and meaningful reflections.

I'm someone who absolutely loves learning. It's a never-ending adventure for me—constantly diving into books, soaking up podcasts, and eagerly absorbing new ideas from every corner. When I stumble upon something fascinating or insightful, it's an electric moment. I feel this surge of excitement bubbling up inside.

And when I learn something new, oh, I have to share it! It's not just about spreading information; it's about sharing the joy of discovery and the thrill of newfound knowledge. Whether it's a practical life hack, a deep philosophical insight, or a simple yet profound way to approach daily challenges, I want others to experience that same sense of enlightenment.

For me, sharing what I learn is more than a habit—it's a passion. It's about connecting with people, sparking conversations, and creating moments of mutual growth.

That being said, I can't really teach what comes naturally to me. I never consciously worked on becoming confident or sharing freely. But what I can teach are the things I actively worked to improve and cultivate, such as the art of complimenting others. You know those people who have a knack for making you feel like a million dollars? They always know just the right words to say, not generic compliments but detailed praises that show genuine appreciation. I've always been captivated by them and wanted to be like that, too. I craved to be the kind of person who notices the intricate details that make each person unique and special, delivering compliments that evoke a genuine surge of warmth and validation. So I put effort into improving myself.

I'm here today not to tell you that I'm perfect—far from it. I'm still a work in progress. I'm here to tell you that change is possible for you, too. You can become a nicer person! You can be like the women you admire! You can become any kind of person you'd like to be!

How did I change? Well, the first step was that I got fed up with my excuses! That's the first step. You must be fed up with your own nonsense.

You have to recognize that the muddy rut you're stuck in is less than ideal, and have the desire to clean off your dirty shoes and step into a pair of clean ones.

You must acknowledge where you are, be ready and willing to give up your own nonsense and excuses, envision where you want to be, and then genuinely desire to make that journey.

You have to want it.

That's the start.

And as I always say, if you want to change the way you react to things, become less moody, or lose weight ... if you want it badly enough, you'll get there. How will you get there? I don't know. Just like weight loss, there's no one-size-fits-all secret pill or diet or exercise routine that works for everyone. A therapist who clicks with one person may not resonate with another. These things are like finding a *shidduch* (match); it often takes trial and error and a whole lot of patience, and you need a lot of *siyata d'Shmaya* (Divine help). But without a strong desire and ambition, you won't persevere through the search and the trying. That's why wanting it, craving it, is truly everything.

I always hated that we were such *tzikuchte mentschen* ("heated" people). I vividly remember arguing with my extended family about it when I was around 17 years old. They often made fun of cold, chilled people, insisting that they weren't so proper, like us. Those people didn't have our touch; they weren't as effusive and gracious when receiving gifts, among other things. But I would counter, "I wish I were that chilled." I truly craved to be like those who seemed so calm. Who cares if we're perceived as more proper when we're also so uptight and often nervous wrecks?

When they looked at me as if I had just said I wanted to be a snail, I explained, "They have a calmer life!"

They argued back, "We are *varim*, warm-hearted. It's not good to be cold."

I responded, "Well, I don't see the glory in being so warm-hearted that you keep overreacting and getting all worked up over every little thing. When a chilled person doesn't want to attend a wedding, she stays home and has a calm night. She doesn't spend the entire night torturing and berating herself for not pushing herself to attend the wedding, like we do."

Even at the age of 17, I disliked certain aspects of my personality. I didn't like how easily I would get worked up, how I argued until I was blue in the face, or how aggressive I could be. That dissatisfaction kept me searching.

Ultimately, I changed because I became fed up. And that, my friend, is the first step.

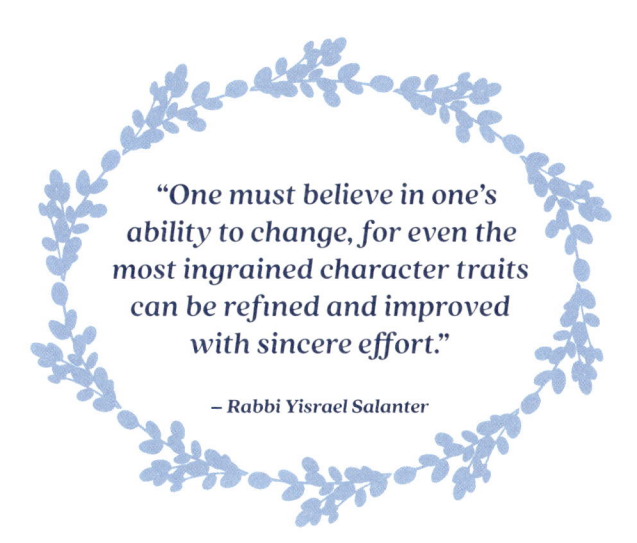

> "One must believe in one's ability to change, for even the most ingrained character traits can be refined and improved with sincere effort."
>
> – Rabbi Yisrael Salanter

THE EX-YENTA

I'M SO STRONG IN MY BELIEFS. I DID MY RESEARCH, I discussed this with so many wise people, I read the *mussar sefarim* (Jewish-based ethics) that support these ideas. That's why I started writing this book—to put my steadfast beliefs on paper.

But now, suddenly, I'm unsure.

My thoughts keep pacing back and forth in my mind. I'm sick and tired of playing devil's advocate with myself for so long.

Dark circles shadow my eyes, remnants of countless late-night writing sessions. I've been pouring my heart and soul into this book for months—actually, years. Every sentence is a reflection of my deepest beliefs, my core values, my understanding of the world.

Lately, my writing has been moving so smoothly, gliding along like those moving walkways in the airport. Fingers flying over the keyboard, thoughts flowing effortlessly. My stream of consciousness coming to life in letters, then words, then sentences—curating an impressive collection of my convictions.

The world outside fades away when it's just me, my thoughts, my classical music, and my MacBook. Everything is in sync.

But then, Skeptic-Raizy pipes up. She's a wise guy, always ready to challenge my convictions with her sharp wit and a knack for constantly finding problems and holes in my reasoning. I mean, I like her; she's pretty smart, she challenges me. She sharpens my ideas. But she also confuses me!

It's usually subtle at first, a whisper of doubt that creeps into my mind. "What if I'm wrong?" I pause, fingers hovering over the keys. The once-familiar confidence begins to waver. The words on the screen blur, suddenly seem foolish ... and I start to question everything.

I lean back in my chair, staring at the ceiling, the questions swirling in my mind. Am I too wrapped up in my own perspective? Am I too idealistic, too hopeful about humanity? Am I unrealistic about our ability to evolve?

I think about the conversations I've had, the debates and discussions that have shaped my beliefs. Have I truly listened to others, or have I been so focused on articulating my own thoughts that I've ignored dissenting voices? I wonder if I've fallen into the trap of confirmation bias, seeking out information that supports my views while dismissing anything that challenges them.

And that's when the ruthless game of playing devil's advocate with the voices in my head begins. And yes—it's ruthless. It leaves no stone unturned, and it keeps throwing stones around in there until it all hurts so bad....

This agony, these moments of uncertainty, of questioning and introspection, are a vital part of the creative process, a necessary step in the journey of forming educated beliefs. I know that embracing this doubt can lead to a deeper understanding of my beliefs and the world around me.

I toss and turn throughout the night, until an uneasy sleep finally overtakes me. I awaken to see rays of a new morning stream a halo of hope into the dim, sleepy room. I take a deep breath, grounding myself.

The doubts are still there, but they're no longer paralyzing. Instead, they become a tool, a means to research, to hear more, and to alter or strengthen my arguments. You see, when she speaks up in there and challenges my beliefs, I get curious, which ultimately leads to clarity.

One of the narratives she keeps echoing is what so many people say: "*Once a yenta, always a yenta.*" But I disagree. I disagree so much that I've spent countless hours on this mission to raise awareness of the belief that we can all be more, that we are all more than just pathetic yentas. We should all strive and work towards living a rich, elegant life!

I think the Torah shares my belief as well. People with fixed mindsets erroneously assume that we can't change our natures. However, our sages tell us otherwise. Our sages teach us that we're given a certain nature in order to improve it. As Rabbi Manis Friedman writes in his book *Creating a Life That Matters*, "A person's nature is just a starting point, not a life sentence." We are never stuck. Life is about this work. Life is full of infinite possibilities for growth.

With renewed determination, I take my phone and type out the following, then promptly post it to my WhatsApp status without overthinking:

> "*Any Ex-Yentas out there?*"
>
> "*Meaning: you used to be a yenta, but worked on yourself and you feel like you no longer are?*"
>
> "*Do you think there is such a thing? Any thoughts?*"
>
> "*I'm doing research for something and would like to ask a few questions... you would be anonymous.*"

That's what I posted one morning after my doubts about this book had grown to the extent that I was close to giving up. And oh, am I glad I did!

After posting that, I got out from under the covers, slipped my feet into my cozy slippers and headed downstairs. I started the hot water kettle and opened the shades. I put a teaspoon of coffee granules into my mug—the pink one. I made myself a cup of coffee and sat down at the kitchen table to sip it.

Then, one by one, I began to read the messages that popped into my inbox. The responses blew me away. I'll start with Shevy's story. This one inspired me most, because it showed that what I believe to be possible is truly possible. Shevy made a 180-degree turnaround.

"Sure, there is such a thing," responded Shevy, a woman I know through business and highly respect. We've had pretty enlightening conversations in the past, from which it was clear that she's a worked-on person.

"I didn't call myself a yenta, but a woman in the know. Now I literally turn down information about other people. I used to be judging and have an opinion about everything; now I'm focused on doing me and becoming the best me."

"Tell me more," I requested.

> *"I grew up in the center of Boro Park. We would sit at the Shabbos meal and look out the windows, and we talked about every person who passed by. On the street, we looked every person up and down. We were so into it. We lived in the center of town, knew everyone's life inside and out—when they go, when they come, what we heard, what's happening.*
>
> *"When I got married, my husband was horrified. He tried to shut me down, telling me, 'This is ugly. This is horrible.'*
>
> *"I had so many arguments with him about this. I tried to convince him, 'Why? It makes life so fun!'*
>
> *"'What's fun about talking about other people?' He was incredulous. 'Until they talk about you…'*
>
> *"He was right. It took me years. First, I worked on trying not to see who was walking around on the streets. At my mother's Shabbos table, I tried to keep the window shades closed, and my sisters didn't like it at all. 'Because you decided to change, you have to make us all crazy?' So I sat on the other side of the table where I couldn't see the window.*
>
> *"It was a whole journey for me. I'm not gonna say that the gossiping stopped completely. I still had certain friendships that were based on the juice.*

"And then came the big nisayon that proved my husband was right when he said, 'Until they talk about you.' We got enmeshed in a whole dirty political story, and my friend wanted all the details. But now I was past that.

"It took a long time for my friend to realize that I was not trying to snub her, but that I was changing. I tried telling her, 'I'm sorry, my life is private, and I want to keep it that way. I don't want to give you a report.' No matter how nicely I said it, and even though she said, 'I understand,' the relationship ended, cold turkey. I lost many close friends over this because they didn't like what I had become.

"When I was going through this murky saga, I had so many temptations to call up women who had been in similar situations, to share and hear details about their experience. But I held myself back.

"My children know that if they come home with a story about someone, I'm not interested. My house now revolves around positivity and self-growth. I became focused on my own house and my own children. I don't know what's happening with others—and I don't care.

"You may call me self-centered, but I would rather be this way than know what's going on in other people's houses. I'm so out of everything. People come and tell me news, and I have no idea what's flying.

"It was an avodas hamiddos for a very long time until it became second nature. Now, I go to my mother, they tell me names, and I'm so disinterested.

"You can definitely work on yourself not to be nosy. And you can channel your curiosity into different things. I'm nosy about the human body, the human mind, human nature. I became interested in different topics, and those are the topics I put myself into."

Another woman wrote:

"Of course yentas can change! Nosy people very often suffer from lack of self-esteem and self-awareness. I'm sure that after healing that, they don't have the need to be a yenta anymore."

Women shared with me how they became fed up with that nagging feeling that would linger in their hearts long after exchanging community gossip. These were women who decided at one point to put down their scalpels, stop dissecting the lives of others, and instead focus on self-examination to see how they could improve their own lives.

They were honest:

"I find that hanging out with shallow people makes you fall back."

> "I'm not a malach (angel). I also enjoy a good scoop every now and then ... but it's 95% self-improvement and only 5% gossip. That 5% is okay because it gives me such an ichy feeling and reminds me why I don't waste energy on the rest."

These women were genuine gems. A rush of respect washed over me—they inspired me so much, I literally got teary-eyed.

Other women shared their stories and perspectives. I can't describe the incredible warmth I felt as I read through these messages and spoke with the women who shared their stories, acknowledging my truth. Their words filled me with a sense of purpose and reignited my confidence and motivation to keep at it.

> "I used to be on the phone, chatting away with everyone ... these days I'm barely interested in other people's lives and no longer spend hours on the phone. I lost lots of yenta friends along the way. I realized that talking on the phone takes up so much mental space that by the time the kids got home, I was literally exhausted. I decided I want to create my own life with my husband and kids, and you know what? Life is so blissful! Instead of wasting time on the phone, I sit and play with my children, who are my life. And I take a yoga class once a week, so I get to meet people and have a social life as well."

Wow, this was relatable for me. My change came about for similar reasons—I didn't want to waste my precious energy on other people's drama. For me, the shift became about channeling my energy in a constructive way, because I want to lead a life I'm proud of.

People always ask me, "You do so much. Do you have more hours in your day?" The answer is no. I also don't have a ton of energy. I'm a homemaker, a mom of little ones and a pre-teen, and a wife. After all that, I don't have much energy left. What I do have, I preserve and treasure. I ration it carefully, and I even take naps.

I definitely won't use up my precious time or energy chatting on the phone for an hour about someone else's divorce that has nothing to do with me. That would be a waste of time, energy, adrenaline, and potential.

My secret to success, I truly believe, is first, Shabbos, which I wrote about extensively in my first book; and second, my mental energy, which I actively work to preserve. I treasure it and ration it like the precious commodity it is.

When people wonder how I manage to accomplish so much, I don't think it's about minutes. It's the energy that they lack. I avoid wasting mental energy on drama or gossiping on the phone. Frankly, I don't see the point of spending the day tethered to another person on the line, listening to them manage their household, talk to their little ones, huff and puff, answer the doorbell, with occasional interjections of *"Nuu ... Vus nuch?* What else?" I find it a tremendous waste of time and energy to breathe together on the phone, waiting for something interesting to happen. I prefer to do my breathwork in privacy, thank you.

> *"Definitely think there is such a thing. I used to be much more involved than I am now. I'm not really interested in knowing about others' lives unless I'm connecting with them personally or they choose to share. I'm more focused on my own life, my growth, and my son. I can't change others, and knowing more about their lives doesn't help me in any way. Realizing and accepting that helped me steer away from the urge to pry."*

In all honesty, there were also some women who responded to my post with hysterical laughing emojis:

> *"There is no such thing! I feel like once a yenta, always a yenta! It's in their blood."*

I heard them. I suppose they knew too many yentas, and not any Ex-Yentas.

Some women thought it was a joke. I find that many see humor in the word "yenta." But it's the last thing I find amusing. If I expressed my reaction to what the word "yenta" evokes, it would be an extremely sad emoji. Just plain sad.

Now I ask you:

Who would want to be such a sad human?

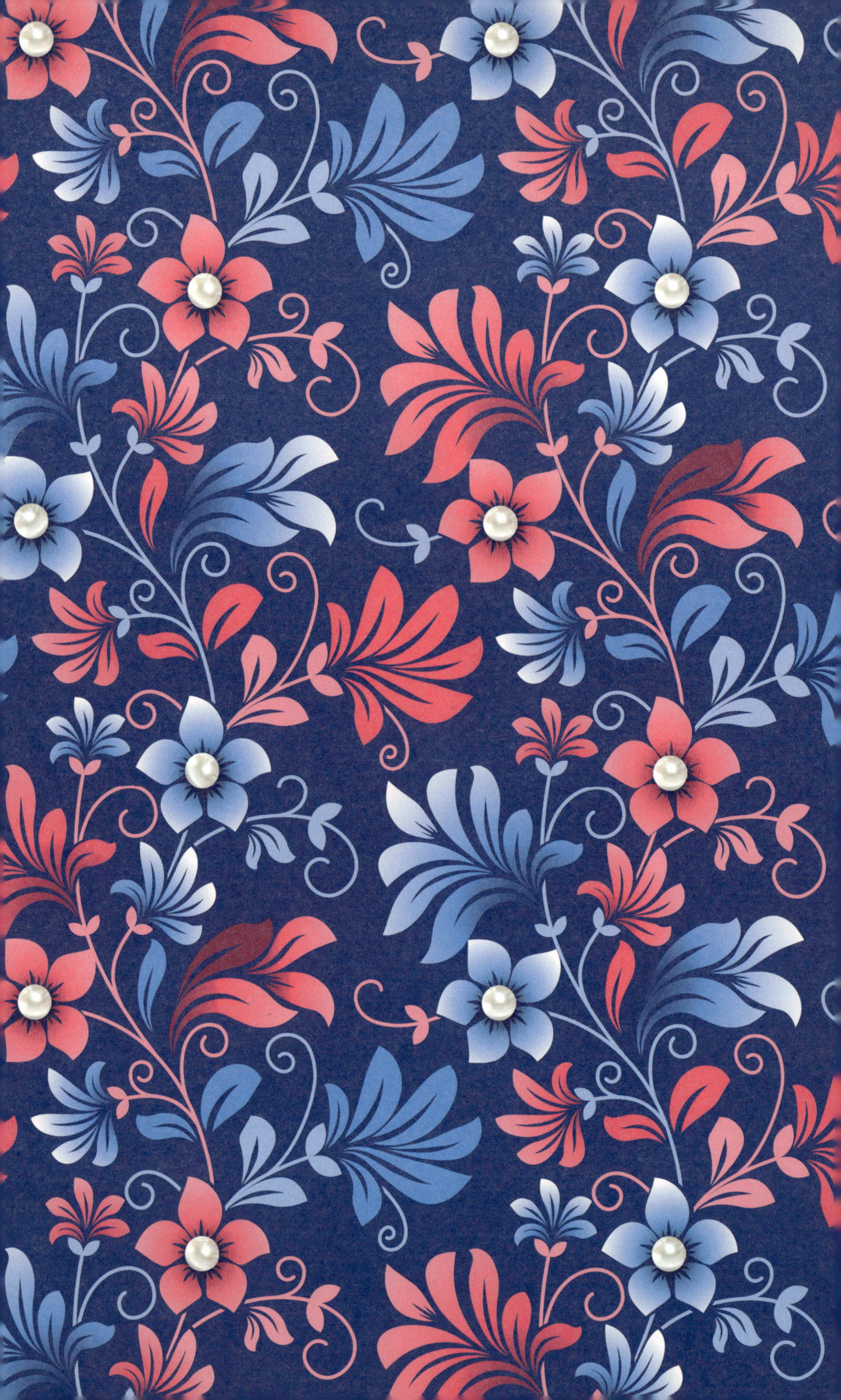

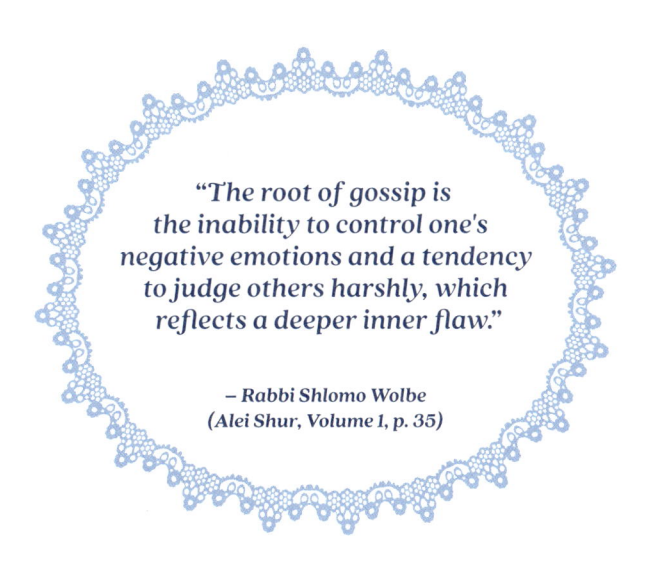

> "The root of gossip is the inability to control one's negative emotions and a tendency to judge others harshly, which reflects a deeper inner flaw."
>
> – Rabbi Shlomo Wolbe
> (*Alei Shur, Volume I, p. 35*)

FROM GOSSIP TO GROWTH

WHEN I WAS GROWING UP, ANTI-*LASHON HARA* campaigns were the hottest thing. Everyone and their grandmother were committing to an hour when they wouldn't speak *lashon hara*. It wasn't just in my school or community; it was simply in style. You would walk into the store to buy a Shabbos robe, and as the conversation with the saleslady got exciting, she'd suddenly shush you, put her finger to her lips, and say, "It's my hour." That's when you realized what you were saying was *lashon hara*. Ugh, it sucked all the air out of the animated exchange!

It was everywhere. I vaguely remember posters and women wearing stickers, and I hoped they would just give up soon because their conversations were dull and filled with small talk. And diets! Women were going on and on about what they ate every day and how they weighed their cottage cheese. I was going out of my mind.

"So, in the morning I wake up, and I have six ounces of cantaloupe and three tablespoons of cottage cheese. Then for a snack, I can have five almonds or two rice cakes, the thin ones, without the salt."

This was the soundtrack of my childhood. Come to think of it, wouldn't it have been a great mental health movement to enforce an hour of no diet talk? An hour without hearing about grapefruit, cabbage soup, or Dr. Atkins would have been pure bliss!

I don't know how long those *lashon hara* campaigns lasted, but I remember them well. And I remember hating it because it was really hard to wait until my friend's hour ended so I could hear the scoop. It was like a social media blackout before social media existed!

This book you're holding in your hands doesn't approach *lashon hara* that way. You're not going to hear the usual discussion. It doesn't focus on the irreversible damage inflicted upon the person being spoken about; we know that already. Instead, it delves into what gossiping does to ourselves and our *neshamah* (soul).

We discuss that haunting feeling that settles in your stomach long after the crowd has dispersed, the unsettling sensation that lingers well beyond the fleeting satisfaction of gossip. We delve into ways to cleanse ourselves of the bitterness that taints our self-image, whether we're staring at ourselves in the mirror or tossing and turning in bed, feeling uncomfortable with how we see ourselves and how others see us.

Because let's not forget that long after the excitement of gossip dissipates, what lingers is a bitter aftertaste … and worst of all, the labeling of those women, who are now notorious for being snoops, tattletales, drama queens, and yentas. Regardless of who we spoke about or how outlandish their behavior may have been, the specific names, situations, and details are no longer relevant. The manner in which we spoke about others now influences how *we* are perceived … and it's not exactly flattering.

In this book we touch on self-image. But it doesn't stop there, because I think the biggest tragedy is the squandered potential. Like those crusts of bread that children often leave uneaten, our *koach hadibur* (power of speech) is the best part! Yet so many women leave it on the plate, only interested in the soft inside. Perhaps they fear biting off more than they can chew—but that's a childish concern. Going out of our comfort zones and trying to improve is where the best is found!

We're naturally curious about others' lives and behaviors, which often sparks the urge to gossip. Curiosity itself is an essential trait to self-growth, but it's crucial to channel it in a positive way. Spending time on gossip sidetracks us from more meaningful activities, hindering personal growth, learning, and the pursuit of positive interests.

My mission is to empower women to recognize that there's a much better way to live. It's not just about our *Olam Haba*; G-d enables us to reap satisfying results from our efforts right here, right now—a life filled with true *sipuk* (fulfillment) and *menuchas hanefesh* (peace of mind).

To begin, we really have to understand the root causes, which can be different for every person.

Let's explore the root causes of gossiping. What is it for you?

Here are some of the most common reasons why women might engage in gossip:

1. To Fit In

Sharing information, even if it's gossip, can help women feel closer and more connected to others. Gossip often serves as a means to create and strengthen social bonds within a group, providing a sense of belonging. In some social circles, gossiping is a normal and expected behavior as women seek to blend in and be accepted.

Many times we share things, even though it's not ours to share, as a way to hotwire a connection with a friend. Brené Brown sums up the unspoken conduct of some women using the well-known quip: "If you don't have anything nice to say, come sit next to me." Many women have what she calls "common enemy intimacy"—the intimacy they have is not real; it's built on hating the same people.

However, gossip offers more than just social bonding; it also provides a sense of influence and manipulation. By sharing specific information, a woman can shape how others perceive someone else.

The paradox lies here: While women may actively participate in gossip circles to feel included and liked, they often overlook that this behavior can also keep them trapped. Constant engagement in gossip can damage one's reputation and social standing. While it may be appreciated by certain individuals, it can also lead to isolation or exclusion from those who value integrity, trust, and respect. If you're stuck in this behavior, you may never attract the attention of women who are growing and can help you grow.

This underscores the importance of surrounding ourselves with the right people who bring us up, rather than down. We'll explore this more in the "Friendships and Friend-Shifts" chapter.

2. Entertainment and Enjoyment

Talking about others' lives can be amusing, entertaining, and provide a break from your monotonous routine. To which I say: Why is your life feeling blah?

Many women gossip out of sheer boredom, seeking cheap thrills. Very often, women engage in gossip because they have nothing better to do, or because they feel so dead and bored inside that someone else's drama makes them feel alive.

Suddenly, they experience emotions they rarely feel in their own lives. A rush of excitement and intrigue fills the void. Their interest is piqued, and they are now hanging on every detail. They are captivated by the unfolding drama, feeling a thrill that contrasts sharply with their usual boredom. The rapt attention of those around them, listening with wide eyes and eager ears, only amplifies this pleasure, creating a sense of connection and validation that is both exhilarating and addictive.

Boredom may seem unassuming and innocent, yet beneath its seemingly harmless exterior lies great danger. Boredom serves as the root cause for many issues.

In the words of the great philosopher Arthur Schopenhauer:

> Man is a compound of needs which are hard to satisfy; that their satisfaction brings little pleasure; that, for the most part, the human race is burdened with sorrow; and that man, if he is left in complete possession of all his senses and is wholly free from pain, must still contend with the problem of boredom, which, as a natural reaction, he is inclined to stave off by means of variety and distraction; thus he is constantly vacillating between the two extremes of distress and boredom.

In today's world, boredom presents psychiatrists with more challenges than even distress, manifesting in growing rates of depression, aggression, and addiction. This pervasive sense of ennui also affects our moral standards and our *Yiddishkeit*. Boredom leads to transgressions and fosters a lifestyle that lacks pride and fulfillment. The emptiness drives people to seek stimulation in unhealthy and destructive ways.

"Existential vacuum" is a term coined by Viktor Frankl, the renowned psychiatrist and Holocaust survivor, in his book *Man's Search for Meaning*. It refers to a condition of widespread feelings of emptiness and meaninglessness in life.

Key aspects of the existential vacuum include:

1. *Lack of Purpose:* Individuals experiencing an existential vacuum often feel that their lives lack a clear purpose or direction.
2. *Boredom and Emptiness:* There is a pervasive sense of boredom and inner emptiness, as people struggle to find activities or goals that give them a sense of fulfillment.
3. *Despair and Depression:* This vacuum can lead to feelings of despair, depression, and anxiety, as individuals grapple with the apparent lack of meaning in their lives.

According to Frankl, the existential vacuum can be filled by finding personal meaning in life, which involves identifying unique purposes and values that resonate with the individual.

Feeling blah and bored is detrimental to our growth. We should be living lives brimming with inspiration and meaning, filled with experiences that make us dance with joy. We should be so intellectually stimulated and deeply engaged in our own pursuits that it's like having a full plate of nourishing gourmet cuisine—there's simply no room or appetite left for the empty calories of gossip or trivial drama.

This belief is at the heart of my message, woven throughout every chapter of this book: to empower each of us to elevate our lives with purpose, substance, and profound meaning.

3. What Else Should We Talk About?

Gossip becomes a default topic when individuals lack curiosity or interest in more substantial subjects. This results in shallow interactions centered around others' lives or trivial small talk. This, to me, is the saddest reason women talk about others. It's heartbreaking to see women who have no meaningful interests or passions.

We live in such a rich world, surrounded by so many points of interest. Our minds are the most intriguing, fascinating organs, capable of observing, storing vast amounts of information, engaging in critical thinking, and magically pulling out the right pieces of information when needed. I can't fathom the anguish of an adult woman blessed with these incredible cognitive abilities who chooses not to use them. I don't believe many women are innately unintelligent, but I do believe many, many women choose to embrace ignorance.

Some women consciously choose not to open their minds to explore, learn, and self-educate. These days, there is literally no excuse! Even if you can't read or sit through a lecture, there are countless other options and different media to learn from. There's so much joy and fulfillment that comes from engaging with the world in a deeper, more meaningful way.

It's never too late to choose growth over gossip, to ignite your curiosity, and to experience the thrill of becoming wiser and more informed as you fill your mind with endless knowledge. I delve more into this in the chapter "*Tafkid* and Talent."

4. Escapism

Gossiping can serve as a form of escape from personal or societal issues. It allows individuals to divert their attention from their own lives and challenges by focusing on the lives of others.

Women often turn to gossip to escape from deep-seated trauma or a haunting sense of emptiness, driven by a lack of fulfillment. When you feel comfortable and good in your own skin, there's no need to run anywhere.

When I hear women venting their frustrations, cursing out the system, and ranting about their mother-in-law, neighbor, or friend's sister, I feel deep sympathy. I just want to go over and give them a hug. Because I know it's not about the person they are going on and on about; they are hurting inside.

When people feel dissatisfied or directionless, they may engage in gossip to temporarily boost their self-esteem, create drama, or cope with feelings of envy or inadequacy. Gossiping provides a sense of importance or excitement, filling a void that comes from not having a healthy self-worth or meaningful life.

An unhealthy, low self-esteem is the foundation here. I discuss healthy self-esteem in the chapter "Rise and Shine" and share how you can improve.

The next time you find yourself engaged in gossiping, pause for a moment and ask yourself:

> *Why?*
> *Why am I doing this?*
> *What am I hoping to achieve or gain from this conversation?*
> *Is this behavior contributing positively or negatively to my relationships and self-image?*
> *How would I feel if the person I'm talking about knew what I was saying?*

> "When we are bullied, it is not just our body that is bruised, but our spirit. The most painful wounds are often invisible, and they are the ones that challenge our sense of self-worth and dignity. To allow someone to be diminished is to damage the image of G-d in which we are all created."
>
> – Rabbi Jonathan Sacks, *Dignity of Difference*

RISE AND SHINE

I was once that moody woman who would wake up in a bad mood every day, the heaviness of another morning pressing down on me like a pile of encyclopedias. The faint light filtered through the shades, but I didn't want the glimmer of sunshine. I was disinterested. I wanted to close my eyes so I wouldn't see the sun, my life, or myself. I wanted to go back to sleep, and sleep for I don't know how long—until I found the desire for the day. Each movement felt like a chore, from the reluctant opening of my eyes to the slow, heavy drag of my legs off the bed.

I tried to pull myself out of the whirlpool of frustration. With a heavy sigh, I would make myself a coffee, hoping the warm brew would quell the storm brewing within me. Then I ate cake. Neither helped much; they just dragged me down more, making me yearn to get back under the covers. I sent off the kids: tights, shoelaces, ponytails, gel, *peyos* (sidelocks), breakfast, sandwiches, mitzvah notes, and bus stops. I forced myself through the motions.

Once the kids were out, the low feeling would hit me with a bang. Ouch! I was mad at the world, and the worst part was that I often had no idea why. It helped when my poor husband said something that ticked me off, when a neighbor was being nosy, or when the bus driver was obnoxious; then at least I had somewhere to direct my anger. It helped when I had someone to blame for my emotional imbalance.

But often I was just a heated mess, and I didn't know why. I can't explain how painful that was. I would be fuming at society, fuming that I had to work—even though I was doing things I theoretically loved. The love was blocked, inaccessible to me.

Why did I have to work at all? It was a mixture of resentment and anger. I didn't want to do anything!

That was the old, moody me. I was an overachiever who would dramatically overreact at every little thing that didn't go my way. A perfectionist with extremely high expectations of this world and everyone in it. I was an obsessive thinker, constantly replaying conversations in my head in which I was speaking my mind. Except I wasn't—it all stayed in there.

Outside, I tried to present as pretty, cool, calm, and collected.

I remember when I was starting out as a makeup artist and hair stylist. I was fuming at my family members who didn't hire me when they married off children. But I didn't say a word. Instead, I tried to fight the anger by overextending myself—I made cheesecakes and salads for their *simchah* (celebration). I wanted to smell like cherries and roses everywhere, leaving only a trail of rose petals and compliments behind.

I was a control freak, a.k.a. Mrs. Moody, and it was pure torture. But you know, being moody isn't just about feeling grumpy. It's about being stuck in a state of low self-esteem and feeling down about everything, especially yourself. Moodiness and low self-esteem feed off each other: when one kicks in, the other follows suit, making it difficult to ever be happy.

Being moody and having low self-esteem are interconnected in several ways. Here's how:

1. Emotional Instability

Low self-esteem can make people emotionally unstable, leading to fluctuating moods. They might have frequent mood swings because they are more sensitive to failure, criticism, and rejection.

2. Negative Self-Talk

People with low self-esteem often speak negatively to themselves, causing sadness, frustration, and anger. This negative self-talk can make their moods change frequently as they struggle with their self-worth.

3. Increased Stress and Anxiety

Low self-esteem automatically causes higher stress and anxiety levels. When people feel they aren't good enough, they keep doubting themselves or worry excessively about fitting in. This constant self-doubt and worry can lead to chronic stress. In turn, chronic stress contributes to anxiety, as individuals become overwhelmed by their perceived inadequacies and the pressure to meet external or internal expectations. This cycle of low self-esteem and anxiety can also make them moody, leading to frequent mood swings and irritability, further impacting their mental and emotional wellbeing.

4. Social Withdrawal and Isolation

People with low self-esteem might avoid social situations because they fear rejection or judgment. This avoidance can lead to loneliness and sadness, affecting their moods.

5. Reaction to External Feedback

People with low self-esteem are more affected by what others say. Even small criticisms can hurt their feelings deeply, and compliments might only provide temporary relief. Sometimes they can't even accept compliments due to their negative self-perception. They often make up stories in their heads, interpreting compliments as patronizing or insincere. For example, they might think, "Oh, she just said that to make me feel good."

6. Perceived Lack of Control

Low self-esteem can make people feel helpless, that they have no control over their lives. This can lead to frustration and irritability, causing moodiness. Despite their hard work, they feel they have no control over their career progression because they believe they aren't good enough to be promoted. When a project doesn't go as planned, they might feel powerless to fix it and become easily frustrated. "No matter how hard I try, it's never good enough." "Why even bother? Nothing I do makes a difference." "I have two left hands." This sense of helplessness can spill over into their personal lives, making them irritable with friends and family, even over small issues.

7. Depression and Other Mental Health Issues

Low self-esteem is often linked with depression and other mental health problems, which can cause long periods of sadness, irritability, and emotional numbness.

Low self-esteem often develops from repeated negative experiences or criticism that can erode one's sense of self-worth over time, especially if you've been a victim of abuse. The more viciously you were mistreated as a child or even as an adult, the more your self-image suffers.

Beneath the surface, I carried suffocating secrets and trauma. On top of that, for at least the first 25 years of my life, I felt profoundly and persistently misunderstood.

Confidence wasn't my issue—I had plenty of that. Unlike confidence, which I possessed in abundance as belief in my abilities, my self-esteem had plummeted. Self-esteem isn't the same as confidence at all; it pertains to one's overall sense of worth and value.

But I persevered. I put on a sturdy pair of waterproof boots and weathered life's ups and downs until the summer of 2017, when I endured an ordeal that shattered me to pieces. It wasn't the worst thing I'd faced, but it attacked my essence, my core, and broke my spirit.

Without going into specifics, I experienced a form of bullying that deeply wounded me, unlike anything I had gone through before.

This wasn't my first encounter with bullying. Throughout elementary school, I endured daily torment, including an incident when "CRAZY RAIZY" was scribbled all over my brand-new pencil case. The class was often divided, with the majority aligned against me. I never spoke about it publicly because it really doesn't haunt me now. Perhaps it's because of my confidence, support from my parents, my talents and hobbies, or the resilience I built in high school. Whatever the reason, the bully eventually apologized after changing schools, and I rarely thought about that period for the next 15-plus years.

High school was better in the bullying department, *baruch Hashem*. But I struggled with feeling unfulfilled and bored, in addition to struggling academically due to my poor memorization skills. I hated high school, though it wasn't due to bullying.

Emotionally, I carried the weight of many heavy secrets that burdened my heart, and I battled with countless inner struggles. I was filled to the brim with questions—about *Yiddishkeit*, practical matters, and more. When I dared to raise some subtle questions in the lessons at school, it didn't go well; the teachers couldn't handle it. They labeled my questions as *apikorsus* (blasphemous) and insinuated that people like me were problematic.

I vividly remember one very sweet teacher. After I asked a question in her lesson, she remarked, "You know, I once had a friend like you. I saw her lately … she went off the *derech*." She said this in front of the whole class.

I probably turned beet red. Outwardly, I laughed it off as if it was the most absurd joke and I couldn't care less. Inside, though, how deeply it hurt. Oh, how I cared.

Still, I have always been driven and determined. The truth seeker in me didn't give up and pursued answers, even when it meant taking the city bus to the Flatbush Judaica store where I could find more open-minded kinds of books (that weren't available in Boro Park) to answer my questions.

During the last week of twelfth grade, in the middle of finals, I got engaged, and joyfully bid farewell to school. Freedom awaited me under the wide-open sky, smelling of sunshine and freshly cut grass. I was filled with happiness and sweet, sweet hope. Ahhh! I was so ready to move on. The torment of school and teachers who didn't like me seemed finally over—or so I thought.

Back in those days, my school didn't publish a yearbook for the twelfth grade. But my class was passionate about it, and we decided to create our own. Though it was a collaborative effort among my class of 31 students, I took on the main responsibility for executing it. I designed the entire book myself, spent hours typing everything up, and laid it all out on my old, clunky laptop which didn't stop crashing. I found a printer in Williamsburg with the best rates and made the trip to deliver my precious files on a CD (since my laptop had no internet access).

I can't explain the *simchah* when those books got delivered, all bound and perfect. The yearbooks turned out stunning, bound in silver covers with our school logo embossed on the cover. I was incredibly proud of how they looked. Since we created them ourselves, they were filled with everything we wanted—inspiration, pictures, creative features, and funny memories. It was a masterpiece that excited us all. I managed the logistics, and each girl paid around $30 for her copy to cover the costs. The yearbooks were distributed at a graduation party hosted by one of my classmates following our graduation.

We all moved on with our lives. I got married the following November and was immersed in my *shanah rishonah* bubble—running from my office job to pick up my husband from *kollel* (institute of advanced Torah study), then to my mother for supper. All was well until one high school teacher somehow discovered the yearbooks and found several jokes about her inside.

To make a long story short, this teacher was furious about it, and she wouldn't let it go. She insisted she wouldn't forgive me until every copy of the yearbook was returned. During the first year of our marriage, various teachers, including the principal, repeatedly called our small, cozy apartment, disrupting our peace. To be honest, the jokes may not have been very respectful, but they were typical school banter—certainly not deserving of such a reaction and harassment.

Although the jokes weren't all mine, I was targeted because I oversaw and directed the project. The teacher's family harassed my husband in *kollel*, and even my boss approached me one morning at the office, mentioning the yearbook gossip circulating in shul—it had become a topic in our community. Thankfully, I had a good marriage (whatever that means in the first few months) and a supportive husband; otherwise, it could have really strained our relationship.

I relied on the coping skills that I, Mrs. Confident, had cultivated and used to navigate through life up to that point. I laughed it off, stewed in it, and even put the principal on speaker so my husband could hear her admonish me.

It was during this time that I faced some health complications, and a doctor told us that it would take a very long time until I became pregnant. I was terrified of the *hekpeida* (grudge), afraid that I wouldn't have children if this teacher didn't forgive me. Despite how difficult it was, I did what was necessary: I pleaded with friends to cooperate in returning the yearbooks.

There were 30 girls in my class. Many laughed it off and were adamant about keeping their copies. They were out of school and weren't willing to let some teacher control their lives.

Since the girls were not willing to cooperate with the teacher's orders, I tried to reason with the principal, offering options that would be more realistic. "We can tear out that page," I suggested, "and if you don't trust us, we can call a meeting of all the girls so you can watch us scribble up those few jokes with black permanent marker."

But the teacher refused to budge. She would not forgive me until she got back every single one of the 30 copies that had been printed.

I had been married for just a few months, and between work and supper, I called my former classmates, tearfully pleading with the girls on the phone, asking them to give back the yearbook. To do it for me. I cried on the phone, doing whatever was necessary to get the job done, so the teacher would forgive me and I could have children. After work, I'd come home to deal with this dreadful school drama. Teachers called to encourage the collection process, and one mother, who had a good relationship with the principal, came to collect the yearbooks from my little apartment.

I was only 19. Despite being confident and seemingly cool, I succumbed to the terror and blackmail. I didn't have the self-esteem and empowerment to stand up for myself. I knew it was absurd, but my focus was solely on starting a family. I had heard stories about the consequences of someone having a *hekpeida* against you, and I didn't want to take the risk.

Eventually, I managed to retrieve all 30 books, and that storm passed. *Baruch Hashem*, I had two lively children, I moved to Lakewood, and a few years went by without much thought of school, teachers, or the drama.

Then, in the summer of 2017, a new incident of bullying began. This time it was more personal. Now I was older; there was more at stake. And I had also reached my limit.

Up until that point, I had been jumping over every bar set for me. But at 25, as a hard-working mother of two young children, I simply couldn't continue. The bar was now set impossibly high, and I didn't have the energy to try anymore.

I felt like I was never going to be done with those who wanted to control my life. I felt like there was no way out.

Self-esteem? There was never a chance to develop any of that. My self-esteem was nonexistent.

That August found me slipping into vaguely familiar behavior without a conscious decision—a behavior of the past, of that dark era I thought I had abandoned for good. It was the kind of behavior reminiscent of my tough teenage years.

I found myself walking for hours, and while you might think that sounds healthy and beautiful, it was nothing like that. That summer I walked, crying uncontrollably like a little child. I found myself listening to the same music I had listened to as a miserable twelfth grader. The songs that were supposed to console me only proved how fragile I was. The notes reached right into my wounded heart, piercing my soul. I was trembling and crying like a baby, listening to the same song that made me cry—on repeat.

Does it seem that I liked the crying? I didn't. It was more like mourning. I mourned my fate and nursed my pained heart.

I remember one day in particular. I had left at 10:00 AM for my morning walk. The tears were falling so fast that I knew I couldn't even pretend to be okay, so I chose to walk in a secluded area where no one would see me. I was crying uncontrollably, my chest heaving with each sob. Two hours later, with a full staff waiting for me in the office, I was puffy eyed and deep in self-pity. I can't describe what these bullies had touched. They had attacked my identity. I felt trapped, like there was no way out.

I thought I was in a good place. I married well; I had a loving husband, two adorable healthy kids, a *chassidishe shteeb* (chassidic home), a flourishing business—and I was a mess. And that's an understatement.

I was being such a good girl. I didn't let a computer into my home. I didn't drive, despite all the challenges I faced as a businesswoman. When I had to attend a meeting in Manhattan, I took a bus to Boro Park, then from Boro Park I took the train to the city. But no matter how hard I tried to fit in, it felt like I was a lost case. I was a *bushah* (shameful), they yelled in front of me and my husband.

I think I'm pretty good with words, but there is no combination of words that can explain how deeply they drilled into my soul. I have a good soul, though I might not have recognized it then. But now I felt as though my fight for individuality and happiness, all the work of high school and the eight years following, had come crashing down in my face. I felt like I was stuck and would be misunderstood forever.

What hurt even more are all the people who knew this was going on and did nothing. All the people who knew what we were going through and just went on polishing their own lives. As they say, the deepest scars are often left not by the cruelty of the oppressor, but by the indifference of those who stand by and do nothing.

Meanwhile, the world was looking up to me as a *chassidishe* role model. I kept getting messages from women who expressed how they started keeping Shabbos because of me. But all I felt was a deep sadness. All I could see were the words echoing in my mind, the words of my bullies: "You're a disgrace."

My shame was so deep. My confidence was a thing of the past.

"What now?" my mind asked my heart. But my heart was too busy grieving to reply. So my mind just stayed there, trapped in a loop of sorrow, listening to the same repeated thoughts about how misunderstood I felt. Life was dark. I felt there was no way to escape the relentless tide of anguish.

Within the deep sorrow of being judged was an intense longing and desire to be respected as every human deserves. Would I ever be able to fully be myself? Would I ever be worthy?

If I wasn't walking, I was working like crazy, trying to push the "you're a disgrace" voices from my mind. Work was the only thing that kept my mascara in place and my face looking pretty. At work I was hitting momentum—my business was flourishing. I would spend ten consecutive hours at work or more. In retrospect, I was running away ... When the children came home from school, I took them to the office, where they would color, make a mess, or drive me crazy—usually a combination of all three.

At one point, when I didn't know what to do with myself anymore, I turned to my Father in Heaven and spoke from my heart that all this *agmas nefesh*, this tremendous pain and suffering, should be *kaparas avonos*, atonement for my sins. I prayed for Him to listen to the cries from my broken heart, keep me and my family healthy and emotionally happy, and make miracles happen.

I had a straight, honest, upfront talk with Him:

> *Tatte, You created me this way. You could have created me in a typical shape that would slip right into the mold perfectly. But You didn't, right? These kochos (strengths) You embedded in me are causing problems, big problems. Eibeshter, You could have created me with an uncomplicated personality that wouldn't intimidate or bother people. You could have made me mild-mannered, in a way that would keep everyone around me comfortable and happy. But You chose my personality. So I'm asking, rather pleading—Tatte, please take care of this personality of mine. Because I want to live, really live. A life of*

constant ache and looming emptiness that no amount of distraction can fill is not living; it's dying.

In hindsight, I see that I was doing exactly what He wanted. I was following His script, and the pain and torture were part of the plan. Every big *askan*, everyone who uses her voice out there, has gone through some version of what I experienced. I've come to learn that it's part of the package.

You see, what I didn't know back then was that your biggest haters see your potential before you even recognize it in yourself. Anyone who invests their precious time and energy criticizing you recognizes that you possess some form of power and influence. No one bothers to bully someone who doesn't matter. It's when you're too big for them that they feel intimidated.

But I didn't realize all this back then. My life looked bleak, and I couldn't see myself ever being happy and content again.

It wasn't only in the radical statements made to my face, but even the little comments from people, here and there … The surprise some people expressed to my husband when they saw me davening in shul on Rosh Hashanah and Yom Kippur. Apparently, they were shocked that I was interested in praying to my Father for a sweet year. I can't actually know what they thought about me, because I never got a copy of their brain files. I only know the comments I heard, the rumors, and the harassing emails I received. Oy, the anonymous emails were bad! The language confirmed they were coming from community people, though I still don't know who sent them.

One of the men who bullied me back then sent an apology through my husband this past winter—a good seven years later. In the heat of it, I remember fuming, "They won't even bother to apologize." But now I didn't need the apology anymore. The biggest bully of them all never apologized, but I don't need it. I put in the work to forgive them a few years ago. I did it for myself—because I wanted to be free.

When that period of bullying finally ended, I tried my best to move forward, but it proved to be incredibly challenging. That winter, I crashed big and hard. I endured excruciating back pain and debilitating sciatica.

I would throw myself in bed, my whole body shaking and throbbing from the *yesurim* (intense pain). Painkillers helped, but only to a certain extent.

There were stretches when sitting was impossible for weeks on end. I spent time on bedrest, enduring a long period where every little physical task felt incredibly difficult. I remember how challenging it was to move my hands to brush my daughter's hair in the morning—it felt like lifting a truck. I broke down in tears midway through, and my husband took over.

As I began to feel slightly better and tried to work from home, I alternated between standing and lying down, because sitting was unbearable. I was then managing social media for a large supermarket, which required me to visit and film in their store. My husband would drive me, as I lay down in the car using a special pillow due to the pain. Despite seeking help from doctors and chiropractors, nothing alleviated the suffering—because the root of it all was emotional.

Thankfully, *baruch Hashem*, I encountered people who guided me through this ordeal. They enlightened me about the importance of caring for my wounded heart, teaching me how to nurture myself back to a positive state. I began the journey of reprogramming my mind and beliefs, paving the way towards healing and recovery.

I started working on my self-esteem daily, a practice that continues to this day. Self-esteem is the feeling that's there with you always, even when you make a mistake or something goes wrong. Now it happens automatically; it's become second nature. But then it took very active hard work.

Today, I see myself as the soul that I truly am—a pure, good *neshamah*. No one, *absolutely no one*, can convince me otherwise. I meditate and connect deeply with my *neshamah*. I am profoundly connected to my Creator and my *tafkid* (purpose). I know who I am—a kind-hearted person with genuine intentions—and I embrace it wholeheartedly!

But I reached this point only through dedicated work on my self-esteem. After I crashed, I started actively working to modify my thinking patterns by reinforcing new messages repeatedly.

In the morning, I would say to myself, "I'm going to work on improving my mood," and I forced myself to see goodness even in areas where it was difficult for me to see it. I nursed my self-esteem by repeating messages like, "I have value," "I am good," "I am really a good person, a pure person, even if some people might not recognize it." I repeated these thoughts day after day.

You see, the only way to acquire healthy self-esteem is through healthy self-talk, which is incredibly difficult for someone who has been continuously bullied throughout her life. No matter how many times she picks herself up and brushes herself off, there's always a little birdie saying, "Perhaps they are right."

The Torah tells us, "*V'ahavtah l'reachah kamocha*, love your friend as you do yourself." But do you really like yourself? Why don't we often like ourselves? Because of all the negative self-talk, much of which was instilled in us.

I worked to repair myself. As lame as it sounds, I actively worked to tell myself:

"I am good."
"I like myself."
"I respect myself for who I am today."
"I don't have to apologize for my feelings."
"No one can blame me or make me feel bad for something I didn't do."
"I am my own best friend; I accept myself wholeheartedly."

Oh, it was not easy being my own best friend during those days. The only way to get there was to treat my wounded heart with kindness—a lot of kindness. And it was so hard.

I felt like a bitter, hurt, aggressive woman, but I created a pleasant, sweet, soft voice in my head, and I forced myself to speak to myself with respect and compassion. I nursed my wounded heart and told myself through tears in my eyes:

"I am very *ehrlich* (honest and sincere)."
"No one can make me feel bad."
"I know who I truly am."

Throughout the day, I trained myself to keep checking in with my feelings to ensure I truly felt good about myself.

It wasn't smooth sailing, I kept falling back. When I made a mistake, as all humans do from time to time, I would fall back into thinking, "Well, I'm *chazer fleish* (pig meat) anyway..." (Yes, I had been compared to *chazer fleish*—one of the flattering compliments they threw into the package.) Despite knowing how absurd it was, deep down it still bothered me and continued to surface.

All it took was a moment I wasn't proud of, and there I would be, telling myself the same horrible things my bullies told me. "They know what they are talking about! You're a disgrace!"

It happened automatically in my subconscious, the emotionally bleeding parts of my brain. Like a little kid, I had to learn the basics—how to handle failure like a healthy human being.

This is a journey that every woman in pain who has faced abuse, has endured hardship, and is seeking solace, must undertake. It's not easy to sincerely praise yourself, to let those affirmations truly sink in, to nurture genuine self-appreciation. It feels super awkward at first. You might even be reading this and making mental excuses, thinking, "*Come on, Raizy, you made sense until now, but aren't you becoming too self-obsessed?*" You might be pulling up all the lessons about *anivus* (humility) you've learned. And that's okay, I understand—because I've been there too.

Talking kindly to yourself might sound like fun, but back then, it was anything but. I was miserable. Telling myself to appreciate who I was, affirming that I was a good person, felt like trying to convince myself the sun was shining in the pitch-dark night. It felt ridiculous. But it's crucial, because it's impossible to shine, to be a truly *ehrlich* Yid, if you believe you're garbage.

Self-esteem is the belief that I have value, that I am somebody. I don't need other people to validate me or give me permission to feel good about myself.

Every person has beliefs. Some people believe they will have a hard life. This belief may be based on past difficult experiences and feel completely valid. However, that belief is how they attract a hard life. The more you dwell over how overwhelmed you are, the more anxious and overwhelmed you'll be. We make all our decisions, subconsciously or consciously, based on these beliefs. It's a huge disservice to continue feeding ourselves these toxic thought patterns, because they are what actually make life difficult.

Looking back, I can see how my low self-esteem kept inviting chaos into my life. While I do wish that I had this understanding earlier—during the time when I was enduring the most excruciating bullying of my life—I am also aware that I possess this knowledge now solely because of that experience.

You see, we are each composed of our thoughts and emotions—every concept, view, opinion, belief, hope, and dream that we've gathered. In your mind, you've curated a specific set of thoughts and emotions. This mental framework, if negative, prevents you from truly seeing your essence and soul for what it is. Unfortunately, many women become so deeply entrenched in their thoughts and emotions that they never move beyond them, never discovering how genuinely pure and beautiful they are.

Time and again, we've seen the importance of recognizing our innate holiness. In a letter from the Lubavitcher Rebbe,[1] the Rebbe writes:

> *There is surely no need to emphasize to you at length that every Jew, man or woman, has a nefesh Elokis, which is a part of G-dliness Above, as explained in the Tanya, beginning of chapter two. Thus, there is no such thing as a small Jew, and a Jew must never underestimate his or her tremendous potential.*

Living with negative self-perception isn't just incredibly painful—it also keeps you stuck. Stuck in life and in your *Yiddishkeit*. You cannot become a *tzaddik* (righteous) when you feel like a *rasha* (evil).

---

[1] From an English letter from the Lubavitcher Rebbe dated 3 Nissan, 5744

Each one of us is holy. As the Baal Hatanya said,[2] "*A yid iz nit er vil, un nit er ken zein upgerissen fun gutlichkeit.* No Jew is willing—and no Jew is able—to remain separate from G-dliness."

And as the Lubavitcher Rebbe said:

> The reality of every Jew is that, regardless of their outward appearance, "even though they have sinned, they are still Yisrael" (Sanhedrin 44a). They have a pintele Yid, which means they neither want nor are able to detach themselves, G-d forbid, from divinity.

> As the Rambam ruled (Hilchos Geirushin, end of Chapter 2)—the true desire of every Jew is to fulfill G-d's will, and what sometimes appears otherwise is only superficial, due to "their evil inclination overpowering them."[3]

Don't fool yourself into thinking that by believing you're not a good person, you're being humble. Playing humble and thinking you are not holy is actually the game of the *yetzer hara*, the evil inclination. Don't fall for it. You are inherently holy.

Our failures, downfalls, and errors are never expressions of our true selves, even though the *yetzer hara* tries to convince us otherwise. It's the moments of elevation, connectedness, and spirituality that express the truth within us. We must focus on these moments and try to accumulate as many as we can, because they reflect our true selves.

Someone once told the Rebbe: "Jews who don't keep Torah and *mitzvos* the whole year and only show up to synagogue on Yom Kippur are merely playing dress up." To which the Rebbe replied: "On the contrary, the whole year they are playing dress up, and one day a year their true essence shines."

If you want to understand how restrictive your self-beliefs are, observe your feelings when you change the narrative. See how it feels when you try telling yourself, "I'm a *tzaddekes* (righteous woman)."

Try it now. I'll wait.

"I'm a *tzaddekes.*"

---

[2] Hayom Yom 25 Tammuz

[3] Sefer Hasichos 5752 vol. 2, p. 384

Do doubts immediately creep in? Do you hear an inner voice saying, "Come on!" or, "Who do you think you are?"

Do you find it difficult to accept? Does it feel unfamiliar or wrong? Does resistance arise instantly? Do you feel silly?

If this happens, understand that there's work to be done. It's not about ego or arrogance—it's essential to reach this place so you can lead a happy life and fulfill your purpose in this world. There's no way around it. If you can't embrace the pure soul that you are, you'll remain trapped in the thick mud of self-doubt and limitation.

When you come up with excuses to avoid this work, you're defending your own blockages. These blockages are adorned with memories of past experiences, making them appear legitimate. However, our task in this world is to transcend these barriers and access the limitless. This work, my friend, is the foundation—the essence of *avodas hamiddos*. It's what we were brought down to this world to do.

If thinking about yourself negatively feels holier than recognizing yourself as the radiant, shining light that you are, you've got a problem. These negative self-beliefs become your prison, and because you're not ready to confront them, you cannot see the purity and potential they are blocking. Our *nefesh* (spirit) yearns for spirituality. It thirsts to actualize its potential, to express itself, and to reveal its infinite potential. Our mission is to provide our *neshamah* with the conditions it needs so it can reveal itself in all its glory.

Your *neshamah's* potential is deep inside, waiting for you to unearth it.

I know it's uncomfortable, cringey work, because I've done it. It can feel like entering an abyss. The closer you get, the more you want to retreat. For many of us, these self-deprecating beliefs are what feel most comfortable, like well-worn slippers that have lost their plushness. We understand that new, plush slippers should feel better, but there's a familiarity and coziness in the ones we've worn for years, molded perfectly to our feet.

We humans are strange creatures in that way. It's kinda the same with a scab that we hope will heal, yet we find ourselves irresistibly drawn to touching it, gently probing with our fingers to feel if there's any dry, flaky part to peel away. We know good and well that we shouldn't keep peeling, we know it impedes the healing process, but we often can't help ourselves.

So often we choose the poor option, and it's not because of lack of awareness. We simply don't want to go there. But here's where I come to gently push you. If you want to shine, you have to go there. When you begin to acknowledge your infinite light, I promise it will all be worth it. Magic happens then. And no matter how aware you are right now, it's only after you're connected to your soul and spiritually awake that you realize just how confined and caged you were. How painful it was to constantly hide within the many limits of your tiny comfort zone.

Here's a list of wonderful results you can expect after putting in the work to improve your self-esteem:

- You no longer see yourself as tiny, vulnerable, and afraid; there isn't this sense of worthlessness.
- You feel like a good person. You love yourself. You have no idea how good that feels—both in the fuzzy sense, and the solid security of knowing that you have your own back. What is self-love? It means you are precious to yourself, and because you're precious to yourself, you are careful not to hurt yourself—physically, emotionally, or even with words.
- You just feel love for no reason. You are all about openness, beauty, and appreciation. You don't need a reason to feel that way; you just do.
- You no longer feel moody all day; instead, you savor the calm and stability of your emotions, resting comfortably in neutral most of the time.
- You experience what it means to have true *menuchas hanefesh*. Life is tranquil bliss.
- You can compliment others with your whole heart.
- You stop attracting negative energy and icy drama. It happens automatically. You don't have to do anything about it. You simply think good thoughts about yourself, speak to yourself kindly, and the world energetically gets the memo.

- You truly shine.
- You are assertive. You stop excusing yourself all day.
- You stop feeling awkward or uncertain about what to say or how to end phone calls ... When you have healthy self-esteem, life is much easier—you can do and say what you want and mean.
- You are no longer desperately arguing for others to see your perspective. You let go of the need to change the minds of others.
- You are unapologetically yourself.

    "I'm sorry if you don't get me. I'm sorry Hashem created me in a shape that doesn't fit into your box. It's not me who's the problem. Hashem didn't make a mistake. I'm not too big; your box is too narrow."

- You respect yourself, and as soon as that happens, the people around you start respecting you too.

The change doesn't just stay in your head; it influences your actions. You stop attracting drama and negativity. You start recognizing your value and the importance of keeping your soul sacred. You become self-protective in the most beautiful way.

One thing leads to another. It doesn't happen in a day or a week, but one day you'll notice your values have changed—you're not interested in wasting negative energy, you're not interested in gossip anymore; you want to keep your beautiful self pure.

It's a beautiful calm that comes only after the storm and the chaos. It's only after going through the darkest of nights that you reach your brilliant light. It's only after overcoming your negative self-beliefs and embracing your inner wholeness and purity that you start waking up each day with joy, your soul basking in the sunshine.

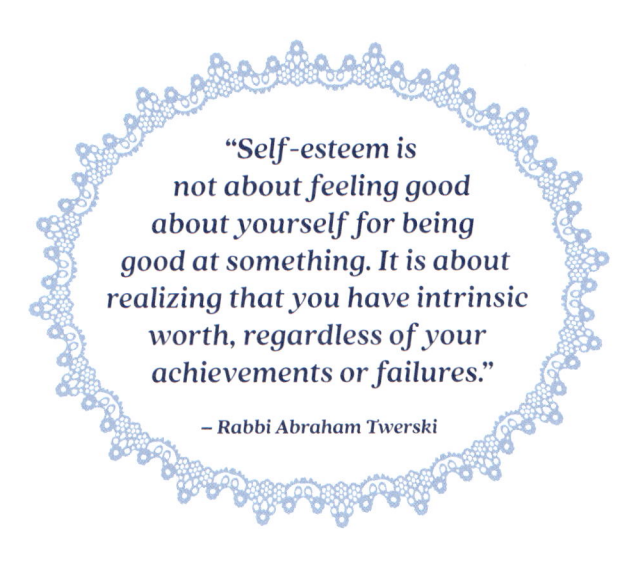

> *"Self-esteem is not about feeling good about yourself for being good at something. It is about realizing that you have intrinsic worth, regardless of your achievements or failures."*
>
> – Rabbi Abraham Twerski

SELF-ESTEEM ESSENTIALS: A PRACTICAL APPROACH

ASK SOMEONE TO SHARE HER *MAALOS*—HER VIRTUES— and watch the color rise to her cheeks, a hesitant smile tugging at her lips. Watch as she starts to fidget, her eyes darting away in discomfort. Embarrassment colors her every gesture, and silence stretches between you. It might feel like an eternity before she finally offers something, often in a small, uncertain voice: "I can sing beautifully," or "I know how to bake."

But ask the same person about her flaws, and prepare yourself to settle in for a long night. The words will come tumbling out with certainty, as if she's been rehearsing this list for years. We are steeped in self-criticism, drenched in it like a soaking rain, more comfortable with our imperfections than with our virtues.

How sad.

"*V'ahavtah l'reachah kamocha*" starts with ourselves. Our relationship with ourselves sets the tone for every other relationship in our lives. We act as mirrors for one another, so if you are someone who often judges yourself, you are automatically more likely to judge others. It's just the way it works. When you become less judgmental toward yourself, when you learn to accept your flaws and mistakes, you automatically start being less judgmental of others. When you recognize and feel that sparkly essence within you, you see it in others, too.

You come to realize that cultivating a healthy self-esteem is not just about yourself. Your infinite light extends to everyone around you, and they all benefit from your healthy self-esteem.

Negative feelings about oneself and a lack of self-love interfere with your ability to truly show up and be present in relationships. When we make nurturing ourselves a priority (and I don't mean manicures and iced lattes), we have so much more to give—and, in turn, can more freely receive. This cycle of abundance creates a solid foundation for healthy relationships and a bountiful life.

Feeling confused or unsure about where you stand?

Not sure about the type of self-esteem you have?

Take this quiz to gain insight into your self-perception and discover areas for potential growth.

SELF ESTEEM QUIZ

1. Do you feel good only when you do things for others?
2. Are you afraid to have a different opinion from others?
3. Can you handle being wrong and admit it?
4. Can you accept a compliment graciously, without feeling awkward or dismissive?
5. Do you tend to put people on a pedestal, seeing them as better than yourself?
6. Is your self-worth heavily dependent on other people's opinions?
7. How do you handle criticism? Do you see it as an opportunity for growth, or as a personal attack?
8. Are you comfortable setting boundaries with others, even if it means saying no?

9. Are you overly critical of yourself, especially when you make mistakes?
10. Are you uncomfortable asserting your opinions or desires in group settings?
11. Do you frequently apologize for things that aren't entirely your fault or responsibility?
12. Do you second-guess your decisions often, constantly doubting your ability to make good choices?
13. Do you feel uncertain or self-conscious about your clothing choices, constantly seeking reassurance from others to make sure you look good and in style?
14. Do you have a clear sense of your own style and preferences, or do you often find yourself unsure about what you truly like when it comes to clothing and fashion?
15. Do you understand and appreciate the unique qualities that make you special and a good person, beyond your talents or achievements?

After answering these questions, if you found yourself nodding along too often, it might be time to sprinkle a little more self-love into your daily routine. Remember, healthy self-esteem means confidently striding through life without constantly looking over your shoulder for approval, stumbling over compliments, or tip-toeing around opinions. Learn to embrace your uniqueness so you can glide through life, dance to your own beat, and celebrate the awesome person you are becoming. You'll get there—I'm rooting for you!

Soulful Self-Care: Nurturing Your Self-Esteem

Let's talk about how you can amp up that self-esteem. There are so many ways for a woman to build that inner sparkle. Here are some awesome strategies to get you feeling like your fabulous self:

1. Discover Yourself

Spend time with yourself. That's the start. You can't tap into your true essence while you're buried in emails, measuring ingredients for supper, or dashing to yet another doctor's appointment with your children. You need to carve out time, moments for yourself to think and work on this. Eventually, it will happen naturally while you're getting dressed, driving, or bathing the children. But in the beginning, it definitely requires more conscious, strategic, and intentionally carving out time.

So, shut off your phone. Find quiet. Listen to your inner voice. Write it down. Talk to yourself: "I'm going to get to know you better."

Give yourself a pep talk. Restructure your inner dialogue to feel happier in the long run. Here are some ideas:

"I like myself. I like myself just as I am. I am kind to myself. I honor and respect myself. I deserve my time and my space—I don't need to escape from myself. Why should I care what others think of me? I am strong in my own right. I support myself. It's okay if not everyone approves of me."

2. Morning Messages

During speaking engagements, I often talk about how I used to be a bitter yenta, waking up in a bad mood every day. I don't go into detail like I did in the previous chapter, but I mention it in passing so women understand where I'm coming from. And every time, women come up to me afterwards, asking for more details. They want to know how I changed because they are struggling too, waking up in a bad mood that defines the rest of their day.

They didn't necessarily go through what I did, but they have their own unique stories. Every woman with low self-esteem has her own cocktail of chaos that brought her to this horrible place, halting her blossoming potential.

How did I fix my moodiness?

It started with speaking to myself every morning. Telling myself: "Good morning, Raizy. I love you. I love you for who you are," and, "I'm becoming a new person."

Start your days off right with positive affirmations. You don't have to say them out loud. You can think them or write them, but give yourself at least a paragraph of positive messages every day. Here are some ideas:

- I like myself.
- I value myself.
- I respect myself.
- I take good care of myself.
- I'm changing and healing.
- I'm happy with myself. My worth doesn't depend on what I do.
- I don't have to do everything or please everyone. When things don't work out, I know it's part of life.
- My inner self is not dependent on success.
- I'm just happy.
- Even if I'm a little sad, I'll make myself happy.
- I respect and accept myself for who I am today.
- I will not measure myself by somebody else's yardstick.
- I am special and unique, and I'll think this way even if no one else believes in me.
- I am my own best friend.
- I accept myself wholeheartedly.
- I don't need approval for being human.
- I have the power to increase my inner happiness and peace.
- I am living life, doing things I want to do.
- I will fill myself with positive thoughts. Depressive thoughts will no longer have room in my mind.
- I will stop running away from myself.
- I don't need anything to make me feel good.
- I feel at peace with my true self.
- I can handle criticism.

3. Practice Self-Compassion

Treat yourself with kindness and compassion, just as you would a good friend. Acknowledge your flaws and mistakes, but also recognize your strengths and accomplishments. Understand that you are a work in progress and that everyone makes mistakes. Be gentle with yourself, offering the same warmth and understanding you would extend to someone you care about deeply. Remember, it's okay to stumble along the way; it's all part of the journey. Celebrate your efforts and growth, no matter how small they may seem.

4. Let Go of Unrealistic Expectations

This is a big one, and it's not easy. Self-compassion involves treating ourselves with kindness, understanding, and acceptance, especially when we face difficulties or make mistakes. One way to practice self-compassion is to recognize and challenge the unrealistic expectations we may have of ourselves. Unrealistic high expectations are a recipe for disaster that often lead to feelings of self-doubt, shame, and disappointment.

We all have these pictures in our heads of the way things *should* be—the ideal. We need to let go of the *should*. Chasing after an unrealistic ideal picture is just being mean to ourselves. It's being our harshest critic and never giving ourselves a break.

Shoulds are expectations. When you catch yourself thinking, "I should really make supper for my neighbor who had a baby," or "I should attend my second cousin's engagement party even when I'm utterly exhausted," it's important to reconsider and prioritize your own wellbeing.

How do we determine what's unrealistic? After all, we all want to give our best and not settle for mediocrity.

Here's the best trick to knowing when your expectations are too high: anxiety!

Your stress and anxiety are gifts. They're your body's personal alarm system that reminds you to check yourself before you wreck yourself. Hashem built it into us, that *ding, ding,* so we know when we've gone too far.

Are you feeling super anxious about your never-ending to-do list and all that still needs to be done? Maybe it's time to reassess what's actually doable within the bounds of 24 hours, considering your stamina, capabilities, energy, and situation. Are you being an overly tough, mean boss to your own precious self? Ouch! Treat yourself like you would want to be treated by someone who truly has your back.

When you're buried under a mountain of tasks, take a moment to reflect. Stop and re-evaluate. Ask **yourself:**

- Can I realistically pull this off?
- If yes, what will the side effects be? Will people around me suffer because I'll be a snappy mom/wife after doing this? Is the gain worth the loss?
- Why am I doing this?
- Why am I helping?
- Do I really want to? Or am I feeling obligated, guilty, or just plain bonkers?

If it's not absolutely crucial and you're not feeling it, give yourself some grace, for goodness' sake! Give yourself permission to hit pause. You are in charge of your life, and if you won't treat yourself with kindness, you can't expect others to cut you some slack.

So many women pile on crazy loads of things to do—just to feel good about themselves. They work themselves to the bone. And when they're done, they're like a ticking time bomb, ready to explode with complaints about how the whole world uses and abuses them. Woman, take a long, hard look in the mirror! Who packs the most work onto your shoulders? Often it's self-imposed. Those *shoulds* you carry aren't real demands from others, and no one cares as much as you do. And even if they do care, maybe it's because of you—because you've been hammering these ideals, high standards, and expectations into their heads.

Imagine a woman beaming with pride as she declares, "In our home, everything is fresher than fresh; we never freeze food." With a gleam in her eye, she continues, "I meticulously iron everything—from our linens to our undergarments—because we're *fein-shmekers* (better) like that."

But after she's poured her heart into baking all her super-fresh goods and ironing every sock, she's screeching, "No one in this house appreciates me! I'm standing here, *shvitzing* (sweating), and no one cares about me."

Woman, who asked you? You set these standards yourself. Somehow, they make you feel like a better wife or mother. But deep down, while you strive for perfection, you often feel miserable, as if these impeccable standards are the measure of your worth. Don't blame others for following the path you've laid out. It's time to reassess and grant yourself the grace you so freely give to others.

By the way, it's never too late to lower your standards! I've done it in several areas of my life. Initially, people might not be thrilled, but after a period of adjustment (for both them and your ego), they quickly adapt. They come to appreciate the new, more realistic standards you've set, which I promise are good enough. They'll come to love the calmer, happier, and all-around more enjoyable woman in their life! Give it a try—it's been tested and proven time and again.

5. Switch to Positivity

It's time to change the narrative. Take note of your self-talk for just one week.

How would you describe your inner voice? Is she encouraging and compassionate, or does she tend to be harsh and unforgiving? Does she acknowledge the complexities and nuances of life's choices, or does she simplify everything into black and white? Does she jump from good to bad without considering the many shades of real-life circumstances?

Is she a doomsayer or a friend?

If you're unsure about the nature of your inner voice, here's a way to figure it out. Imagine your best friend saying the things you say to yourself.

For example, if you called your friend in a panic because you just realized it's Rosh Chodesh and you forgot to dress your son in a white shirt for *cheder*, what would she say? Would she berate you: "You're an irresponsible and terrible mother. Your son must feel so ashamed in his green shirt, and he'll be scarred for life because you can never get your act together." Or would she respond with empathy: "Oh, that must make you feel bad. It happens to all of us at some point. Don't worry about it; your son will get over it."

We women often beat ourselves up over such trivial matters. Oy, the many unrealistic expectations that we impose on our fragile hearts! Would you ever dare call others stupid, fat, lazy, or a schlimazel? I really hope not.

It's heartbreaking how tough we women can be on ourselves! We absolutely do not deserve that kind of negative self-talk. No one does, especially *nashim tzidkaniyos* (righteous women)!

Why does it matter how we talk to ourselves, you might ask? Who cares if we're a bit tough on ourselves? You might even think it's better to foster a sense of humility. But low self-esteem is often fueled by negative self-talk, and vice versa.

Here's what you need to do. Identify and challenge the negative thoughts and beliefs that contribute to your low self-esteem. A crucial part of this process is learning to reframe your mind and perceive yourself and your actions in a more positive light. When you catch yourself criticizing your perceived flaws or failures, swap those thoughts with more positive talk. For instance, if you find yourself thinking "I'm so stupid," try replacing it with, "I made a mistake, but I'm capable of learning from it."

Or think about when you've been running around all day, finally sit down on the couch, and then remember something else that needs to be done. You don't want to get up to do it right then. You think to yourself, "I'm so lazy!" No, woman! You are not lazy; you're simply exhausted.

This is something I personally struggled intensely to change. I used to unfairly brand myself as lazy, which isn't a kind term. Changing this didn't happen overnight; every time I caught myself calling myself lazy, I had to stop and correct my thoughts. "No, I'm actually far from lazy. I'm simply exhausted! Look at everything I've tackled today. I'm only human."

6. Choke the Guilt

Let's tackle another great friend of negative self-esteem: guilt.

Guilt is not a sign of virtue. It's an avoidance behavior that prevents us from establishing healthy self-esteem. The more we accept our real selves and our imperfections, the less guilt we'll harbor.

Often, guilt arises from negative self-talk. We might feel inadequate for not meeting our own high expectations or those imposed by others.

For example, let's say I decide to take care of myself and not attend my cousin's wedding in Boro Park because life has been hectic lately. I'm not sick, everything is fine, and I'm perfectly capable of traveling to the *simchah*. I love my aunt dearly, but I decide not to attend the wedding because I've been out every night this week, it's been hectic at work, and I need one calm night at home to maintain my sanity. A quiet, peaceful evening when I can unwind from the day and go to sleep on time.

What would happen?

I would make the decision to stay home and not go to the wedding, and then spend all night eating myself up with guilt. "Come on, you could have exerted yourself more—you should have gone," "That's what family should do." (Note the *shoulds*!)

Do you realize how crazy that is? I stayed home to be calm, but I was anything but calm. I stayed home so I wouldn't be overwhelmed, but I was overwhelmed with guilt.

"I don't always have to be so *voil* (well-behaved)" was an affirmation I had to learn to tell myself when I was doing the work. Because every other minute, I would feel guilty for not being a nice enough human.

I remember getting nervous from a neighbor who would barrage me with questions. "Are you Pesach cleaning?" she asked one morning, while I was still bleary-eyed and taking my child to the bus.

"Huh?" I asked. I was tired, rushing my heart out and just overall discombobulated.

"Well, I see your garbage cans are overflowing," she said.

I felt a surge of nerves right then. "Stop counting my garbage and keep your nose in your own tissue box," I thought, irritated. Mumbling something about my husband organizing and throwing out things, I made it clear I wasn't interested in continuing the conversation and hurried back inside. Once indoors, I couldn't shake off the feeling of unease. Ugh, I was too snobby. My response wasn't kind or patient enough. I was overly curt.

"But she really got to me," I argued with myself. "What more could I have done?" "No, I shouldn't let people get to me like this," I countered. "I need to improve my *middos*." The conflicting thoughts were battling inside me, leaving me utterly confused and with a pounding headache. Both sides inside me seemed so valid.

"I don't always have to be so *voil*" was an affirmation I told myself to stop the internal fighting and shut down the noise. "I don't always have to be so *voil*" was what I told myself every time I was beating myself up with guilt for not reaching my saintly standards. We are all human. "We don't always have to be so *voil*."

At some point, we have to surrender and accept that we won't always be able to behave perfectly, as much as we might wish to. Sometimes it's possible, but this time it wasn't—and we need to accept that. Guilt is unproductive.

And speaking of guilt, let's give some TLC to the monster: Mom Guilt! *Raaaa!* I know, right?

First things first, let's set the record straight: if you're haunted by mom guilt—that's a sign you are a good mom. Those bad moms you're petrified of becoming—*they* don't feel guilty!

That being said, we still don't want mom guilt, or at least we want to minimize it as much as possible. Mom guilt tends to rear its head from negative self-talk, where moms beat themselves up for not meeting their own or others' expectations of what a good mother should be and do. (See? That sneaky word *should* is always lurking around!) This toxic self-dialogue can turn into a guilt fest, complete with shame, self-doubt, and enough stress to make a circus juggler drop the balls. In short, it's a recipe for distress with a side of existential crisis!

As a mother, I've always wanted to be present for my children and spend quality time with them. However, as a working mom, there have been moments when I've felt an overwhelming sense of guilt for not always being able to do so. I remember when this feeling flared up especially strong on one occasion, and I poured out my heart to my mother on the phone, telling her how I worry that my children will grow up without enough memories of me being there for them.

My mom listened patiently and then reassured me that my children were not missing out on anything. "Don't think the non-working moms necessarily spend more time with their children. Don't fool yourself in thinking that if you weren't working and spending more time with your children, you wouldn't feel guilty ... because then you would feel guilty about something else."

After that conversation, I began actively noticing all the little moments I spent with my children, moments I had never noticed or appreciated before—when I massaged and bathed them, sang to them, or played frisbee with them on Shabbos afternoon. I made a mental note of those moments, and each time I acknowledged them, a warm, fuzzy feeling enveloped me.

Let's replace Mom Guilt with Mom Joy! We need mandatory positive reinforcement for moms, because it changes how we perceive ourselves, leading to better self-esteem and a positive impact on our children. Instead of dwelling on the times I can't be with my children, I now focus on the times I can. This shift in perspective may seem small, but it has profoundly boosted my confidence and self-worth as a mom.

To conquer guilt, when those guilty feelings crop up, ask yourself the following:

Am I dwelling too much on past, agonizing events?
Am I taking responsibility for things beyond my control?
Is this guilt based on my values or someone else's expectations?

It's time to loosen the grip of guilt and embrace our humanity with open arms. Give yourself the green light to be wonderfully human, flaws and all. If we don't cut ourselves some slack, who will?

7. Stop Apologizing

Assertiveness is a cornerstone of self-esteem work, where the focus shifts from constant apologies to self-assuredness. Assertive women don't feel the need to defend themselves.

Apologizing for minor things that don't require an apology, or just using the language, "I'm sorry if this sounds silly, but..." stems from a lack of confidence or a fear of displeasing others. Constantly excusing ourselves for our existence or choices diminishes our self-worth, reinforcing negative beliefs about our value.

Embracing assertiveness means valuing our opinions, needs, and boundaries without guilt or hesitation. It's recognizing that our thoughts and feelings are valid, and we have a right to express them confidently. Plus, assertive people get respect.

This shift not only enhances how others perceive us but also strengthens our self-esteem by affirming our worth and agency in every interaction.

Oh, and while we're at it, let me give you an example by talking about one of my pet peeves: people adding an "LOL" to a comment they texted but feel unsure about. They add the "LOL" to soften their statements or to appear less serious, fearing that their genuine thoughts might be too direct or might not be well-received.

Adding an "LOL" to a text comment when unsure reflects a subtle form of insecurity. It's a way of preemptively diffusing any potential discomfort or awkwardness that the message might cause. This behavior can be seen as a reflection of not fully owning one's thoughts or opinions. And as I always say, if you feel the need to add "LOL," perhaps reconsider texting that comment altogether!

For someone working on self-esteem, recognizing and reducing such behaviors can be empowering. It's these small things that really help reprogram your mind and ways of thinking and feeling about yourself.

Assertiveness in communication, without the need for constant validation or appeasement, is key to building self-esteem. It's about trusting that your thoughts and feelings are valid and worthy of being heard, regardless of how they might be received by others. By letting go of the need to cushion every statement with "LOL" or obsessive excuses and/or apologies, individuals can cultivate a stronger sense of self-worth and confidence in their own voice.

8. Find the Good Feeling Inside You

Do you work yourself to the bone for that good feeling? We often push ourselves too much in pursuit of a good feeling. Always remember, your value is not in what you do; it's in you.

My biggest accomplishment is not feeling the need to accomplish. One of the biggest mind shifts for me was realizing, "I don't need to work so hard for a good feeling."

Students often push themselves to the brink, believing that perfect grades and endless extracurricular activities are the keys to happiness and self-worth. Entrepreneurs sustain themselves on the adrenaline rush of continual advancement and acclaim in their careers, often seeing these as the pathway to feeling fulfilled and good. This relentless pursuit often drives them to burn the midnight oil, shoulder burdens beyond their limits, and inadvertently sideline their personal lives in relentless pursuit of professional success.

But wait, there's a plot twist! Building healthy self-esteem isn't about scoring perfect As, collecting gold stars, or landing top clients. It's about trading the external rat race for an internal spa day of contentment. Picture this: instead of hustling for that next fulfilling high, you're lounging on a hammock of self-assuredness, sipping a cocktail of pure inner peace. Ahhh! Now we're talking. Let me tell you, ladies, clocking into healthy self-esteem is just refreshing!

When you dig deep and unearth the good feeling inside yourself, magic happens. You realize that happiness isn't waiting at the end of a to-do list, securing the top client, or receiving a perfect performance review. It's right here, in the way you think, smile, and sing your heart out when no one's watching. It's the feeling you get when you think of your *neshamah*, your precious *chelek elokah m'maal*—you, a piece of G-d Almighty Himself. If you want to feel good, you don't have to go buy ice cream, organize another closet, or sweat through finishing a task. You just have to go inside yourself to the magic that is you, the creation within you—your innate awesomeness.

9. Build Your Support Squad

Surround yourself with emotionally healthy individuals who radiate positivity, support, and upliftment. This is essential, though often challenging. Seek out friends who aren't just great at entertaining and partying, but who genuinely want the best for you and can shower you with encouragement and validation like confetti. (Read the "Friendship" chapter to learn how to find those friends!)

10. Practice Self-Care

Looking after yourself physically, mentally, and emotionally is key to boosting self-esteem. This could mean ensuring you get enough sleep, eating nourishing foods, staying active, and doing things that bring you joy.

11. Embrace Your Awesome Self

Practice self-acceptance and give yourself a standing ovation—complete with a round of applause and a bouquet of self-love! This involves letting go of the need for perfection and learning to appreciate ourselves and our quirks.

I remember when I was 28, asking a 40-year-old how she felt about her age. Her eyes lit up as she told me she felt better than ever. While her skin may have been prettier in her twenties, she didn't miss the uncertainty and chaos of that time. Now she knows and loves herself, she told me. She doesn't obsess over trivial things and has learned to embrace who she is.

I approached a few more mature women I respect and asked them the same question. They all gave me similar answers. I was blown away, replaying their words countless times in my mind.

That's when my perspective changed. I thought, "Why do I have to wait until I'm 40 to stop being bothered by the nonsense in life, and to embrace my flaws? What if I could learn to love myself unconditionally now?"

Why must I wait to be unapologetically myself and wear what I like? No, I'm not waiting! That's when I started wearing only what I like—more tailored suits, colorful sweaters, and I cut my wigs short, the way I like them.

When fans approach me and I don't recognize them, they assume it's because I'm popular. But the truth is, I've always had a hard time remembering names, even of my first cousins. If my memory was any worse, I'd probably be able to plan my own surprise parties. I used to talk about my bad memory from time to time, and I'll admit, it's mostly to protect myself. But no more! I will no longer apologize for not remembering someone who attended my crowded wedding 14 years ago. While you might have a photographic memory, I don't. And I'm not sorry for it. I'm done apologizing and excusing myself all day.

I will no longer excuse myself for not always being in the mood to socialize outside with neighbors. With a job that demands intense focus, when I come home all I crave is a moment to catch my breath. All day, I dream about unwinding alone—it's the incentive that keeps me going and motivates me. (Plus, I've got to figure out how supper's going to magically appear.) I won't apologize for being busy or exhausted. I refuse to push myself to be outdoors like everyone else if it means I'll turn into a grumpy version of myself. And hey, I won't apologize for safeguarding my energy and living life in a way that fits my personality.

I will no longer feel guilty for not remembering your name. I'm done nodding and pretending I know who you are, only to later embarrass myself when the truth comes out. I'm finished fabricating stories and excuses to mask my self-imposed guilt. No, I don't know who you are, even though your daughter was on my daughter's bus seven years ago, or you met me once in Brenda's big dressing room. No, your name doesn't ring a bell, even though you went to school with my mother and once borrowed orange juice from my grandmother. I've been blessed with many gifts, but a photographic memory isn't one of them.

Believe me, I've spent years making up nice stories customized to what each person wanted to hear, but it didn't come from a nice place at all. I love storytelling, but I'm done with the fiction. Yes, I'm blunt now, and I kind of like it. I enjoy being able to walk into a store and confidently say, "No, I don't like that," even when it's the hottest style, and the saleslady is trying to convince me why I should like it. It's liberating to assertively dismiss trendy pieces with a simple, "Nope, not my style."

I love the way I navigate life now. I enjoy being Mrs. Classy, polished and proper most of the time, but I might surprise you with my quirky and unfiltered side if I feel safe to be myself. You can't just stick me in one personality file; I refuse to flatten myself out just to fit neatly into a category of yours. I'm a compilation that's worn and torn in places, marked and highlighted in many others. I'm overflowing with colorful neon tabs, each one representing a different aspect of who I am. This is me.

Do you know what happens when you stop worrying about what others think of you? You get to dance, to sing at the top of your lungs, to be comfortable, to laugh, to play, and to create like crazy. You get to be yourself and all that you were meant to be. And you know what? Some people won't like it, but it won't bother you much once you've tasted the sweet freedom of living the life you're meant to live.

There you have it: eleven strategies to build your self-esteem. By incorporating these core strategies into your daily life, you can gradually build a stronger sense of self-esteem and improve your overall wellbeing. Remember, building self-esteem is a process that takes time and effort, but it is worth the investment in yourself.

I'm still working on myself. Each day is its own unique story, filled with challenges and distractions. But here's the beautiful part: just being aware of this journey can take you further than you ever imagined. Just wanting to change and feel comfortable in your own skin, the desire to truly embrace who you are, is a powerful start. If you crave it and believe it's possible, you're already on your way to getting there!

All my life, I prayed for calmness, peace of mind, and happiness. But what I realized after I crashed is that peace of mind and happiness don't just land in your soul. They don't arrive with a stork or in dollar signs. Achieving a peaceful, deep, meaningful life takes active intention and effort. I pray that Hashem grants me the strength to continue working on myself, my self-esteem, my attitude, and my soul.

My life's greatest accomplishment won't be found in the many things I've built with my bare hands—not in my books, my channel or my business. Not even in my home or my children. My greatest achievement will be in the mind shifts I've painstakingly constructed with unwavering commitment within myself, even when it seemed like everything was falling apart. It's in the mind I've filled with positive thoughts, the beliefs and attitudes I've nurtured, and the perspectives I've cultivated.

It's in the ability to see my *heilige neshamah* (holy soul) for what it truly is, and to genuinely appreciate the essence of the life I've been granted.

These mental and emotional victories are the hardest and most significant accomplishments of my life.

So, my dear reader, every time you reframe your thoughts, every time you work on your self-esteem, you are working on your *middos*, girl! Remember that all those battles, all those years, all those mini victories are molding you into not just a calmer, happier you, but a *tzaddekes*. I wish I could make you feel this as deeply as I do right now.

My hope is that when the next challenge arises for you, you will sense the warmth of our Father in Heaven beaming with pride as He looks upon His beloved daughter, bravely taking another step forward, despite all the obstacles and difficulties she faces. Another step towards her radiant light; another step closer to Him.

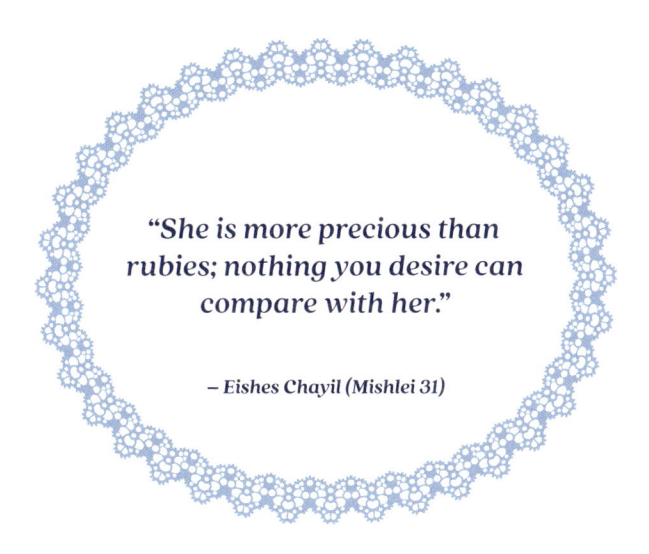

> "She is more precious than rubies; nothing you desire can compare with her."
>
> – *Eishes Chayil (Mishlei 31)*

LIKE A LADY

WE'VE ALL ENCOUNTERED A VERSION OF HER. Her allure is undeniable. The way her eyes sparkle with intelligence and confidence, the subtle curve of her smile. Every inch of her is meticulously curated. She knows how to put herself together … and how! She makes it all look effortless. Her makeup is natural-looking, present but not overpowering. Her wig has every hair "sitting in their places, with bright shiny faces…" She looks flawless.

And then there are her clothes—oh, her clothes! They whisper tales of class and impeccable taste. Tailored to perfection, they drape her silhouette with an elegance that is both understated and commanding. So chic!

While others are scurrying around and constantly adapting their wardrobes to ever-changing trends, she walks around like a lady, picking out her timeless pieces. She moves through life with the poise of royalty; there's fluidity to her movements. The way she dresses, and the way she is, is rooted in a deep understanding of who she is and what she stands for.

There's this magic about her…

Although she may not conform to current fads, she epitomizes mastery in dress, leaving an enduring impression of refinement and sophistication. And although every piece of her looks perfect, she's not obsessed with fashion. She comes across as an intelligent woman who successfully pursues her interests and talents. You can't help but respect her and take her seriously.

It's more than just her physical appearance; it's the essence of her being that captivates us. There's a depth to her character, a quiet strength that shines through every gesture and word. She exudes warmth and kindness, making everyone around her feel valued and cherished. In her, we see more than just a woman of impeccable taste; we see a beacon of grace and dignity—the essence of a truly elegant woman.

She's out of a fairytale, but totally with the program! Whether we admit it openly or harbor the feeling secretly, there's an undeniable desire to be just like her. You can't help but yearn to exude that same self-dignity.

Each of us, as Jewish women, serve as ambassadors of grace through our choice of dress, the warmth of our words, and the kindness we extend to others. We all long to embody this essence, to present our precious *neshamos* with regality and carry ourselves with the dignity it deserves. But often it feels like chasing a dream. Even when we witness some women mastering it, we place them on a pedestal of unattainability, thinking, "She's different … I'm just an ordinary schlump. If only I had her figure, her style, her personality, or her financial means…"

For many of us, it seems too elusive, too daunting, too complex. We see her. We admire her. Yet we dismiss her achievements as unachievable, as if elegance is encoded in some women at birth.

Here's where we're mistaken. When we encounter a woman who impresses us, who exudes refinement; when we marvel at someone's eloquence or elegance—it's not a cue for dismissal. She has entered our lives for a reason.

It's a universal truth that most women inherently yearn for elegance. *Yofi*, beauty, is a gift bestowed upon us by Hashem. This appreciation is far from shallow or vain; it's our sacred power.

Yes, we can and should aspire to be like her. That doesn't mean to mimic her exactly, but to be inspired by her and reach for our own beautiful potential. We are all ladies, and we should all carry ourselves as such.

There's often guilt attached to the natural desire and appreciation for beauty that we have as women, to the extent that many try to stifle it. Women often believe that by choking these beautiful desires, they will be able to attain a higher spiritual existence. Women may also veer away from beauty in an attempt to be more *tzniusdig*, which is unfortunately a very common misconception—and a painful one, I must add.

The opposite is true. Hashem granted an appreciation of beauty especially to us women, because it is a tool to achieve our destiny.

While physical desires may present challenges to a man's spiritual journey, especially when focused on Torah learning, this is not the case for a woman. For us, connecting with our natural inclinations, whether through dressing modestly with grace and respect or by nurturing and beautifying our homes, is how we find fulfillment in our purpose. It's important to remember that indulging in these desires shouldn't mean getting lost in materialism all day, yet if we use them as a means to an end, we make all of Hashem's splendor truly shine!

"A woman who abstains from involvement in the physical world is destroying the world" (*Sotah 20b*). A woman's journey isn't about battling against the physical, but embracing it in her sacred task of nurturing her home. When she suppresses her desires, she loses touch with her feminine essence, leaving herself disempowered and disconnected.

When a woman embraces the understanding that Hashem created her with intention, embedding within her the tools to fulfill her true mission, she realizes that her innate desires are perfectly aligned with her purpose. No longer does she need to spend energy suppressing or battling against herself. Instead, she can gracefully channel these energies and beautiful desires into her sacred work, letting her step into her position like a queen, leading to truly magnificent outcomes. A wellspring of joy and positive energy flows from her, radiating warmth and love to her entire family.

We're about to unravel the secrets of what makes up a truly elegant woman. Fear not, there's no squeezing into corsets or lace gloves involved—not even a curtsy! It's surprisingly down-to-earth, because let's face it, elegance is not just reserved for royal blood—though as Jewish women, we've all got that in our DNA too!

Consider this your crash course. I'll do my best to break it down in simple, everyday language.

But before we dive in, let's address a few disclaimers for those who are dismissing all this as superficial, like cotton candy fluff. The substance of what I'm teaching here won't dissolve at the slightest touch of skepticism. So, for the eye-rolling skeptics in the room thinking that all this fancy-schmancy talk is inauthentic or shallow, this isn't just sugar-coated sweetness. Many people who aren't familiar with elegance think of it in stereotypical terms and associate it negatively with snobbery, inauthenticity, and rich aloofness. That's often due to narrow-mindedness or associations. If you grew up knowing a nasty Mrs. Trainwreck who dressed up as a madame in pearls, no wonder you're turned off.

So, let's start with...

What Elegance is Not

❧ *Elegance is not just about looks.*
Perhaps the biggest thing people fail to realize is that elegance isn't just about aesthetics, and it's not shallow. The values of true elegance actually work hand-in-hand with the values of personal growth, maturity, and self-respect.

❧ *Elegance is not inauthenticity.*
Just take a look at where our misguided #Authenticity #KeepingItReal culture has led us. We see viral "real people" showing up on social media crying in their pajamas. Now, there's nothing inherently wrong with crying or wearing pajamas (or nightgowns, for that matter). But any woman with a shred of self-respect shouldn't be comfortable presenting herself to the world like that—especially not *bnos malachim* (royalty)! Unfortunately,

we've reached a point where people use "being themselves" as an excuse to indulge in bad manners or habits.

Why is authenticity always equated with sloppiness? It's disheartening that some believe having manners and dressing nicely is synonymous with being inauthentic. You can remain true to yourself while also embracing the aspects of your personality that appreciate a particular aesthetic or mannerism. Be yourself, just refined. A more sophisticated, gracious version of yourself. Why settle for anything less?

No, you won't dress or act the same way when you're at work, at a *simchah*, or at home. I sure hope not! But guess what? That's all part of your charm. You can still bring authenticity and realness to every situation. Whether you're dolled up or keeping it comfy and casual, just remember your worth as you adapt to the different roles you play in every setting—all while staying true to the fabulous person you truly are!

I often receive questions from stay-at-home moms who feel trapped in a cycle of neglect, their days blending into one another without much flair. They yearn for the elegant aura of other women they see, but can't shake the feeling that such grace and style are out of reach. They watch as these women glide gracefully through life's social gatherings, whether it's work meetings or lunches with friends, while they remain confined to the roles of homemakers. They don't just feel unattractive; they feel destined for a life without the elegance and vibrancy they long for.

I always tell them, "Just because you're home playing with your kids on the floor doesn't mean you have to look and feel like a schlump." You can look very good at home, too. Elegance doesn't equal makeup or a wig, per se.

I always advise starting by wearing head coverings that suit your face. Many women don't look good in a tiny snood that's sliding off their heads, especially if they have a big face. Try on several options and see what makes you look your best. I find that *tichels* (head scarves) complement and enhance the faces of most women, and they are so fun to have in a variety of different shades and prints, keeping things fresh and matching them to your outfit. I'm not talking about the snug lycra bandanas; I'm talking about gorgeous scarves with body.

Nowadays, you don't even need fine-motor skills to tie them prettily. There are so many gorgeous pre-tied scarves available. Buy them in colors that complement your skin tone. If you don't wear makeup, keep that in mind when shopping; buy a color that will add to your face, not make you look washed out or flushed.

It might take some trial and error. But I know so many women who look like queens in their homes, clad in chic soft tops and lightweight skirts that fit well but are not too clingy, with coordinating tichels that add a pop of color and fashion to their look. They infuse excitement and style into their daily routines as homemakers by embracing a diverse palette of colors and constantly refreshing their looks. These women embody a charming blend of looking classy, warm, and cozy as they move with ease from one task to the next. Yes, our appearance significantly influences our self-perception, and ultimately our performance.

Different situations call for different versions of yourself, and you have the choice to embrace each one with its unique expression of authentic elegance. You're not more real if you stroll to the grocery store covered in flour or baby vomit, just as you're not inauthentic if you grace a wedding in makeup and heels. Neglecting or disregarding your appearance doesn't make you any more authentic!

You'll encounter some women who portray elegance in an inauthentic manner, who overidentify with their looks and use fancy clothing to mask their insecurities. As with everything in life, it's about finding the right balance and having the right intention.

Everyone has a persona that she uses to interact with the world around her, and that's not a bad thing. We all need a filter, a social mask, to be decent human beings. Imagine a world where everyone ran around uninhibited, saying and doing whatever they pleased, driven solely by impulse. It wouldn't be pretty. Despite the current trend of glorifying #unfiltered authenticity, filters are actually extremely necessary to navigate social interactions without causing offense.

Elegance is not stiff behavior.
It's natural, graceful fluidity. If you're dressed beautifully but with a rigid posture, resembling a soldier on parade, that's not elegant. We aim to be

proper, but not to the point of overly rehearsed or scripted interactions, lacking spontaneity and genuine emotion.

We don't want to look like that 5-year-old wearing lipstick who's hyper-aware of it, afraid to eat and move her mouth. If you can't wear lipstick and still smile broadly and talk, then skip the lipstick. Elegance is about natural grace and charm, so it should fit you like your favorite pair of shoes.

Elegance should be tailored to suit you, incorporating your personality traits, preferences, tastes, and values, while still embracing your imperfections and vulnerabilities.

Elegance is not about chasing perfection.
It's like adding a pinch of spice to a dish to bring out the flavor. We're in favor of refining those subtle details to embody the poised and elegant women we aspire to be. But let's not get too caught up trying to be Little Miss Perfect. We want that perfect balance between sophistication and spontaneity!

Now, without further ado, let's dive headfirst into the enchanting world of elegance!

The Elegant Woman

1. The Way She Dresses

It's not all about dress; it's deeper than that. But it certainly starts with the way you dress. You can't help it. It's the way of this world. The way you dress is the first impression you give, and first impressions are crucial.

There's always this argument about the *penimiyus*, the inside of a person, versus the *chitzoniyus*, the outside. And whenever this debate comes up, there's always at least one woman arguing that outward appearances are not that crucial, that we as a society put too much emphasis on it. There's always at least one woman busy explaining (usually in defense of her choices) that though she might not dress so modestly, though she might appear to be more modern in the way she dresses, she is really so spiritual and so connected to Hashem.

It's absolutely mind-boggling how some people believe they have the ability to figure someone out based solely on their appearance. Why automatically assume the guy in a police uniform is a cop? Maybe he's really a firefighter, for all we know! And who's to say that the woman rocking a short wig and a hat is *chassidish*, while the one in a jeans skirt and a wig down to her behind isn't? How dare some people make such wild assumptions?

Let's set *Yiddishkeit* and the Torah aside for a moment, and let's discuss this like the smart, intelligent women that we are.

We live in a world where smart people choose to work within societal norms and not against them. In every community and society, there are rules and norms. Human beings, by nature, are judgmental, and when we meet someone, how she dresses is the first impression we get regarding who she is. How she dresses is what we see first, before she even opens her mouth to speak.

Picture this: someone waltzes into an important business meeting with hair so greasy it could double as a salad dressing and sweatpants that have seen better days. Despite possessing the brains of a rocket scientist and offering the best ideas and deals, chances are his image would be marred by the grime of his appearance. It's like trying to savor a gourmet meal served on a trash can lid—the presentation matters, folks!

Now, I understand if this feels a tad vain or superficial to you, but let's face it: showing up in a crisp, well-fitting suit automatically screams, "I've got my act together!" and conveys professionalism and seriousness about the meeting.

You can flaunt your qualifications and commitment to the project until tomorrow, but showing up looking like you belong at the gym sends a message of carelessness and disrespect. Sorry, that's just how the cookie crumbles in this wild world of ours!

If you want to dress in a way that doesn't signify self-respect and self-dignity, that's fine. But don't expect people to assume you are something you don't appear to be. If you want to dress in a way that's not *chassidish*, that's fine, just don't be offended when someone asks you if you understand Yiddish or assumes you're not *chassidish*. I've encountered this countless times. Women are shocked and bothered that someone they met assumed they were not *chassidish*. They are incredulous and go on and on about how very *chassidish* they are, how proud they are to be *chassidish*. Sometimes I want to challenge them: if you're so proud to be *chassidish*, why don't you dress like it?

Here's a super-genius life hack.

Think: What would you like to be associated with?

Dress that part. Dress the way you would like to be regarded.

When we work within societal rules, aside from being a mature and smart choice, there's also the aspect of the way we dress affecting the way we behave. Let's take a UPS guy. When he's wearing his UPS work uniform, he will automatically act more professional and polite. If you get him upset when he's not wearing his uniform, he might respond in a nasty way. But when you say the same thing to him when he's wearing his uniform, he will respond more carefully. He's on the job now, representing UPS. He has to be careful.

Our outfits work their magic in shaping our demeanor. Wearing the right clothes is like donning a superhero cape, but with the added bonus of pockets for your phone and snacks! So, dear ladies, let's learn to dress for success, both inside and out.

∽ *Be modest:*
An elegant woman is modest. And I'm not just saying this from a Torah, *tznius* perspective. Look at the world. Look at the royal family; look at how serious businesswomen dress. If you want to be respected, you have to first respect yourself. Wearing a super thin T-shirt fabric dress that boldly outlines every contour and curve of the body, or walking around with a long slit up the center of your skirt, while your legs play peek-a-boo with the world … I'm sorry, but that doesn't exude dignity.

Tznius is not just about adhering to rules and covering specific areas. *Tznius* is really about self-dignity. Take those oversized tent dresses that were fashionable not too long ago. They weren't immodest in the least. However, you'll never see Kate Middleton wearing oversized clothing, no matter how trendy it may be. It's simply *s'past eer nisht*—it's beneath her. She knows she's worth more than that. That's the attitude our girls need to feel like royalty.

Don't obsess:
An elegant woman just is. She is less about talking and more about doing—not preaching, just being.

There are women I know who practically have a full-time job shopping, chatting about clothes and brands non-stop, living and breathing fashion. You might picture them as the ultimate fashionistas, owning one jaw-dropping piece after another, but let me tell you, reality is often a comedy. I know some of these women quite well, and it's ironic. The sheer amount of time they dedicate to hunting down and discussing their two new outfits...

It's like that woman who discusses the *upsherin* she's planning a full year in advance. The planning is endless—she doesn't stop talking about all the details! The color palette, the decor, and the bags she's ordering for the *pekelach*. You eagerly anticipate this grand *upsherin* event, only to arrive to something that looks like your weekly *shalosh seudos* with *pekelach* and pretty napkins. Have you ever experienced this? Well, I have, and I encounter this a lot with women who don't stop shopping and dwelling on their looks, the brands, what's in, what's coming in ... With all that hype, you'd expect them to be looking like Princess Diana herself!

Personally, I'm constantly curating an endless array of looks and accumulating a plethora of clothes to accommodate my frequent filming and photo shoots, particularly for my *Inspired Living* show. You know how much energy women put into their appearance at weddings because they feel they'll be on display? Well, I'm on stage every other day, and I care about how I look and come across. Fashion is a significant part of my career and life—plus, I just adore it. I probably won't ever hire a personal stylist because I absolutely love putting together an ensemble. There's an exhilarating sensation in achieving the ideal harmony between colors, textures, and styles. The decision between wearing the blazer open or closed, or choosing between a pleated skirt or a straight skirt ... You'd be amazed at how a certain pair of earrings can throw off an entire ensemble, while the subtle sparkle of stud earrings can infuse just the right amount of glamour and sophistication. And let's not forget the shoes! The choice of footwear has the power to either elevate or deflate the overall look.

These delicate details might seem trivial, but each one can change the entire look. Just closing two buttons of the cardigan and pairing it with a smaller necklace can make the whole outfit look so much better compared to wearing the same cardigan open with a longer necklace. There's an immense satisfaction that comes with nailing the perfect combination that suits you best. Fashion isn't just a fun passion for me; it's an art form.

Yet, if you consider my life as a whole, fashion doesn't consume a significant portion of my time or energy. Ask my mother, sisters, and friends if we ever discuss clothes. Rarely. I simply stroll into the store, pick what I like, then head over to the seamstress. You can call me *geshikt*. I'll accept the compliment, and also tell you that it's not just me: it's Mama, it's genetics—and a G-d-given gift.

But although I may be *geshikt*, I think those who are not will do better when they become aware of how cheap it sounds when you talk about fashion, clothing, brands, and wigs all day. If you're obsessing over clothing, you're expending way too much energy to be classy. It's just not classy.

Elegant women relish the finer things in life, but they never let themselves become obsessed. Whether it's clothing, food, or anything else, obsessions are cheap. Elegant ladies are not obsessed with materialistic things; they never let them rule their lives or define their identity or personal values. An elegant lady cares to dress well, but knows her value is innate and comes from within and the work she has done.

Elegant women do things for themselves, not to impress others. Even when they give back, they do so discreetly, without any need for grand gestures. For them, elegance is all about discretion. They have no interest in flaunting their wealth or proving anything to anyone. Showing off is often a sign of insecurity, and elegant women rise above such behavior.

❧ *Look effortless:*
Elegant women never overdo it!

Looking effortless is all about balance. If you're wearing an elaborate beaded dress, it's best to keep your wig short or styled up, and as simple as possible. Pairing an intricate beaded dress with studded shoes and an elaborate curled hairstyle, with long locks cascading over your shoulders, adorned with all your bling, is simply too much! It's not refined; it's gaudy and ostentatious. Being overly elegant is not elegant at all. Elegant women keep it minimal—refined and respectful.

Even if they possess the most exquisite jewelry, they don't feel the need to flaunt it constantly. They pair statement necklaces with simple tops and understand when to skip the necklace altogether. You don't always have to wear jewelry. If your outfit features a bold collar or detailing around the neck, a simple necklace or no necklace at all suffices. You don't need to wear everything you own all at once; elegant ladies grasp the concept of less is more.

A surefire way to look chic and sophisticated is to stick to solid colors, focus on high-quality fabrics rather than prints, embrace clean lines, and opt for fine jewelry and accessories.

An elegant woman never overwhelms with too much perfume or strong scents. Similarly, she doesn't pile on makeup—no overly bold eyebrow tattoos, heavy eyeliner, or cakey foundation. It's essential to hone your makeup application skills; if you're not proficient yet, it's better to wear less makeup or none at all. Heavy makeup can give off an aggressive, artificial, or aged appearance.

❧ *Be unique:*
Truly elegant women don't settle for boring or dull looks. They don't follow the crowd, not because they consider themselves superior, but because they embrace their unique, personal style. Elegant women understand what works for them individually—the colors that flatter their complexion, the styles that complement their body type and highlight their personality.

It's not about spending hours searching for something no woman has ever worn; it's about taking what you wear seriously and not mindlessly copying and pasting. It's about knowing what you like and what looks best on you, which you learn from trying on different things and looking in the mirror!

I want to wrap up the dress category by sharing what my friend Chiena always says: we have a responsibility not just to dress modestly, but to look fantastic while doing so! After all, you're here to inspire others in your thoughtful choice of modest dress. You're not inspiring anyone when you don't look good.

2. The Way She Speaks

An elegant woman speaks with grace, poise, and confidence. She chooses her words carefully, avoiding gossip or crude language. Her tone is gentle yet assertive, and she listens attentively when others speak. She communicates with kindness and respect, always mindful of the impact her words may have on others. Her speech reflects her intelligence, sophistication, and inner beauty.

ॐ How she speaks:

In *Parshas Yisro*, Hashem instructs Moshe to address the Jewish nation: "So you shall say to the House of Yaakov, and speak to the children of Yisrael..." Based on the Midrash, Rashi explains: "'Say to the House of Yaakov'—these are the women, whom you should address with soft speech. 'And speak to the children of Yisrael'—this refers to the men, to whom you should expound with words harsh as sinews."

The Torah is presented to women with soft speech because it aligns seamlessly with a woman's innate nature, allowing her to absorb its truths effortlessly and naturally. A woman's task is to let her natural feelings come out, which automatically brings Torah into her home. This involves being in touch with her inner self and her heart, which are already in sync with Hashem's will.

I read a beautiful *vort* (Torah insight) in the book *Rachel's Tent* by Tamar Taback:

> Just like Hashem gave the Torah with soft speech, an act that was filled with His trust in the essential spiritual nature of women, we likewise know that we are aligned with our higher selves when our speech to

those around us is soft. Soft speech is the most powerful expression of a woman who is in tune with the intrinsic feminine nature, while at the same time demonstrating her belief in her power to influence, as it says, "Divrei chachomim benachas nishma'im, the words of the wise are gentle and are therefore heard." (Koheles 9:17)

Rivka Malka Perlman is a world-renowned speaker and educator who addresses various topics for women, including self-growth and marriage. I had the honor of filming an episode with her on the power of femininity, which is featured on my *Inspired Living* platform. Rivka Malka speaks in soothing tones, using nurturing language and demonstrating listening skills. In this powerful episode, appropriately titled "Soft Strength Secrets," she shared many gems that deeply resonated with me. However, what inspired me the most was this:

When she discussed femininity, I asked her, "When I think feminine, I think soft spoken, which you're the perfect cover girl for ... What if someone is more aggressive and this doesn't come naturally to her?" (I was reflecting a lot on myself here, as I tend to be aggressive by nature, and my life's work has been to mitigate this tendency.)

Her response swept me away. "First, I'm not so soft spoken," she asserted. I was reluctant to accept that. "I'm really not," she reiterated.

She then shared how her mother had tried to encourage her to behave more like a lady growing up, mentioning that "a lady wears a slip," but she preferred combat boots and considered herself more of a feminist and masculine.

"But when I think of you, I think of a lady," I remarked.

To which she replied, "That's a compliment, because I've learned the beauty of femininity. My natural place is muddy." She explained that her current demeanor took active intention and effort. She is naturally messy, opinionated, and chaotic. She enjoys debating people, but has now discovered the joy of embracing the feminine.

Rivka Malka shared many amazing and impactful ideas in our conversation, but what struck me the most was her revelation that the qualities she now embodies did not come naturally to her. I was so inspired that after the cameras stopped rolling, I continued discussing this with her. (The conversations I get to have with these fabulous women before and after we film are invaluable! I should keep a diary of these off-camera vulnerable interactions and perhaps publish a book of them one day.)

I explained how I'm always enchanted when I listen to these beautifully feminine speakers who speak softly, like her and Rebbetzin Yemima Mizrachi. They put me in a trance, and I know I can only aspire to speak like they do. Rivka Malka explained that she's sure she intimidated some women when she began changing, because she used to be even softer until she found her comfort level.

Then she exclaimed, "Raizy, I'm sure you've changed, too, since you started speaking."

Indeed I had. However, the change was more about altering how I speak from a professional standpoint. I wanted to sound polished. I wanted to sound passionate and dynamic, but not like a yenta screeching her opinions on the park bench…

We chuckled, and she understood me.

What lingered with me long after our conversation was over is the beautiful truth, with the proof I witnessed with my own eyes. The power that we hold within us is that we can each metamorphose into the women we admire and dream of becoming.

What she speaks:
An elegant woman refrains from gossiping, especially in public, and certainly does not engage in it proudly. Such behavior is beneath her dignity.

If only we could cease gossiping solely for altruistic reasons, recognizing the pain it causes our Father in Heaven to witness His children behaving in such a manner toward one another. If only we can stop gossiping out of pure kindness and empathy for one another. We're all aware of the harm gossip can cause—how it can damage relationships, reputations, and trust.

But I say, if we can't find it in our hearts to change for others, let's at least do it for ourselves, out of self-respect. Remember,"*Mitoch shelo lishma, ba lishma*" (*Sanhedrin* 105b). Actions that are started for selfish reasons can evolve into selfless ones over time.

Let's begin with ourselves and pave the way for a more compassionate world. It's a different starting point, but it can guide us towards the same journey of self-growth and the ultimate destination.

Here's a quick list to kickstart your awareness. Next time you're tempted to pass on gossip, keep these thoughts in mind:

> *It's holding you back from your awesomeness:*
Gossiping about others diverts focus from what we truly want in life. Engaging in gossip detracts from progress toward personal goals. Simply put, talking about others is a big waste of time.

> *It invites negative energy into your life:*
Every time we're negative about someone else, that energy affects us, too.

> *It's projecting your own flaws:*
Judging others reflects our own insecurities. Criticizing highlights the parts of ourselves we don't accept.

> *It reveals a lack of trustworthiness:*
Those who talk to you about others, talk to others about you. Those who indulge in gossip may lack respect for you and might share your private conversations with others. Continuous gossiping can strain relationships and erode trust. People may be less inclined to confide in someone known for spreading rumors or engaging in gossip.

Remember this when you are the one sharing a scoop about another person. Although the listener is all ears, she might simultaneously be making a mental note to herself that you cannot be trusted!

> *You become what you consume:*
We all know this to be true with the food we eat. If we consume junk, the negative nutrition settles into our bodies. This idea applies to everything we take in through all our senses, including

the songs we listen to, the media we consume, and the topics and conversations we engage in.

You really need to ask yourself: Do I want to be a dramatic yenta? Or a polished, intelligent woman? If I aspire to be an intelligent, classy woman, it won't happen by watching garbage TV or spending a good part of my day discussing someone else's divorce or dwelling on some blogger's life. Gossiping is unflattering, to say the least!

3. *The Way She Treats Others*

Elegant women exemplify respect in their interactions. Etiquette and manners are important. Their demeanor and code of conduct demonstrate class! Elegant women have *mentchlichkeit*.

Etiquette is not just about carefully placing that fabric napkin on your lap and saying please and thank you. There's also a crucial aspect of social etiquette, which is essential for anyone who wants to be respected. Social etiquette involves being genuinely respectful and sincere in your interactions with people, speaking as though you mean it. It's about having refined and respectful communication, which, in this day and age, takes on a whole different form.

We may be in touch with people all over the world and not meeting face to face as often. We might be emailing more than talking on the phone. However, just because technology has changed the mode of communication doesn't mean that social etiquette goes out the window. An elegant woman recognizes that there are still basic rules of *mentchlichkeit* (the qualities of a good, decent, and honorable person), including when emailing and texting. She always introduces herself with her full name when reaching out to a new person and avoids using text lingo or excessive slang, especially in formal emails and interactions with people who are not close friends.

Exhibit A:

Woman #1 texts the following:
"R U going into Boro Park tonight?"

Woman #2 texts the following:
"Hi, this is Chavi Klein. I got your number from my sister-in-law, Esty Klein. I would like to know if you're going into Boro Park for your cousin's wedding and if you would be able to take someone along as I'm looking for a ride."

Now, tell me which woman sounds like a *mentsch*, and which one comes across as an inconsiderate yenta who doesn't value the norms of polite communication?

Exhibit B:
Woman #1 sends an email:
Subject: Job
I would like information about the job opening. Is it f/t or p/t?

Woman #2 sends an email:
Subject: Inquiry About Job Opening
Hi,
My name is Leah Stein. I saw your post about a job opening, and I am interested in learning more about the position to determine if it is relevant to me. Could you please provide more information? Is the job full-time?
Thank you so much.
Best regards,
Leah Stein

Which woman comes across like a *mentsch*, and which woman comes across as unrefined—*heimish* (not in a good way), flighty, and careless?

Guess which woman's email I don't even bother responding to?

Seriously, I always wonder why this person thinks I'm going to take the time to respond when she didn't take two minutes to write a proper email. I don't need lengthy *megillos*; I'm fine with a casual email, but I'm not engaging with a woman who lacks proper *mentchlichkeit* because she's not someone I'm ever going to hire.

This may seem elementary, but unfortunately, I encounter this carelessness every day. It seems some women really lack awareness. I could literally publish another (long) book with examples of how this issue keeps playing out!

Today's communication is different. We don't walk three miles uphill in the snow to someone's house to ask a question, and we don't send telegrams that take three days to arrive. Yes, we text, but we still have to act like *mentchen* and come across decently, especially if we want to be taken seriously.

Another way an elegant woman demonstrates refinement and respect is—tact! An elegant woman understands the importance of respecting others' privacy. She's never nosy. She doesn't ask too many questions. She understands what topics are appropriate to discuss. She just has tact!

When someone has tact, it means she possesses the ability to handle delicate situations with sensitivity. She knows how to navigate conversations and interactions thoughtfully, avoiding causing offense or discomfort to others. Tactful individuals choose their words carefully, considering the feelings and perspectives of those involved, and finding appropriate ways to address difficult topics or issues without causing unnecessary friction.

Tact might not come naturally to everyone, but fear not, it is a skill that can be learned and developed with practice and self-awareness. It involves understanding social cues and developing empathy and effective communication techniques. By really caring and wanting to change, observing tactful individuals, and consciously adjusting her behavior, anyone can improve her ability to handle delicate situations with sensitivity.

An elegant woman demonstrates tact not only in her interactions with others, but also in what she reveals about herself. She never overshadows her grace by sharing too much. There's a delicate balance between being authentic and oversharing. While it's important to speak one's truth and show vulnerability, elegant women refrain from airing their or their family's dirty laundry. Sharing impulsively or succumbing to emotional outbursts is unbecoming, not part of their refined demeanor. Instead, they share with careful consideration and intention.

Consider Prince Harry, for example. Despite his royal background, his recent public airing of family grievances has been perceived by many as lacking in elegance.

4. The Way She Fargins Others

Elegant women celebrate the success of others with genuine joy and grace. They never succumb to jealousy, bullying, or mean-spiritedness.

There are two types of jealousy: malicious jealousy and positive envy. Malicious jealousy drags you down, leading to gossip, unkind words, and attempts to undermine others. Positive envy motivates and inspires you to strive for more.

An elegant woman knows only positive envy. She warmly embraces the achievements of others, viewing their success not as a threat, but as a beacon of possibility. When she sees someone else's luxurious ideas or accomplishments, she feels invigorated and inspired, never spiteful.

Elegant women are uplifted by the success of those around them. They take joy in the beauty and creativity others bring into the world and use it as motivation to reach their own goals. They understand that someone else's success doesn't diminish their own potential; instead, it highlights what is achievable. An elegant woman knows that by *fargining* others, she enriches her own life with positivity and inspiration.

5. The Way She Preserves Her Energy

Elegant women do not waste their energy on drama.

Engaging in frequent conflicts and disputes is a telltale sign of someone who enjoys stirring up trouble, a trait far from refined. Such behavior often hints at deeper insecurities and unresolved personal matters. In contrast, elegant women gracefully sidestep drama entirely.

While the occasional feud may arise—after all, we're only human—elegant women choose their battles wisely, always tone it down, and distance themselves from recurring drama and overly dramatic individuals.

6. The Way She's Always Improving Herself

Elegant women dedicate themselves to nurturing their emotional wellbeing and consistently elevating their standards. They wholeheartedly acknowledge their areas for growth and actively seek ways to better themselves, not just for their own fulfillment, but also to positively impact those around them. With a deep sense of responsibility, they take ownership of their own challenges. They don't point fingers or place blame at others. They do the work that they were brought down to do—they work on their *middos*!

7. The Way She Remains Open-Minded

There's nothing that signals more class and elegance than being open-minded and non-judgmental. Think of the stereotypical yenta—what comes to mind is someone judgmental and gossipy. We strive to be the opposite of a yenta. And that opposite is a lady—an elegant lady.

Elegant women never look down on people who are different. Truly elegant women never feel superior because of their elegance. They are never snobbish. They remember that people who are not elegant are not lesser; they simply have a different way of being.

Elegant women appreciate diversity. They understand that for some, living a simple, modest life is what brings them true happiness (see the "Open Hearts, Open Minds" chapter for more).

Moreover, elegant women understand the importance of respecting others' beliefs and choices. They recognize that everyone is entitled to their own opinions and lifestyles, and they refrain from imposing their own beliefs on others. Instead, they foster an environment of mutual respect and acceptance, embracing the richness of diversity in thought and perspective.

8. The Way She Receives

An elegant woman knows how to accept a compliment with grace. She won't respond to a compliment with, "Nah, this old thing..." While some women deflect compliments or attribute credit elsewhere in an attempt to exhibit modesty, an elegant woman recognizes that this behavior isn't modest at all. An elegant woman knows how to receive a gift and accept a compliment, not just because she's confident, but because she's in tune with her femininity and understands that receiving is her special feminine strength.

Receiving is one of the most powerful tools that we women have been granted. This holds especially true in our relationships, whether in marriage or between peers. Though we are often groomed to be givers and may resist being seen as needy, an intelligent woman realizes that receiving is essentially the most honorable form of giving!

When a wife receives graciously, it allows her husband to be his best self, tuning into his inborn masculinity and manifesting his fullest potential. Simultaneously, it nourishes a woman's soul with the pleasure and energy she requires to create her *mikdash me'at*.

Among friends and family, when a woman graciously accepts what is given to her, whether it's a compliment, a gift, or an act of kindness, she not only acknowledges the thoughtfulness of the giver but also validates their desire to contribute positively to her life. This act of receiving with warmth and appreciation creates a deep sense of fulfillment for the giver, affirming their worth and significance in her life. Feeling appreciated and valued, the giver is inspired to continue giving. This fosters a beautiful cycle of nurturing generosity, where every act of kindness is embraced with genuine gratitude, sparking even more acts of benevolence. Like ripples in a pond, this kindness extends far beyond the initial exchange, growing richer and spreading wider with each heartfelt interaction.

An elegant woman understands that receiving is not taking; it's giving. When you push away a compliment or a gift, you're rejecting the giver, often making them feel unappreciated, undervalued and foolish. An elegant woman recognizes that people give compliments and gifts because they want to make the other person happy or feel good, and the *mentchlich* thing to do is to accept with gratitude. When she receives a nice gift, she doesn't respond with, "You didn't have to," because that's not polite or considerate. After all, people don't generally give because they *have* to, but because they *want* to express their thanks, happiness, or other overflowing emotion. An elegant woman, even when taken aback because she didn't expect such a gesture, responds gracefully with, "Oh, wow, you are so nice! This is so thoughtful! I'm looking forward to enjoying this!"

An elegant woman is all about grace, making those around her feel valued. She receives like a lady, responding with the kind of warmth that shows the giver she is genuinely appreciated.

An elegant woman gets out of her own head, gently releasing control, and warmly embraces the kindness that others shower upon her. She envelops herself in their warmth and generosity, cherishing it—because she understands that this is exactly where it's meant to reside.

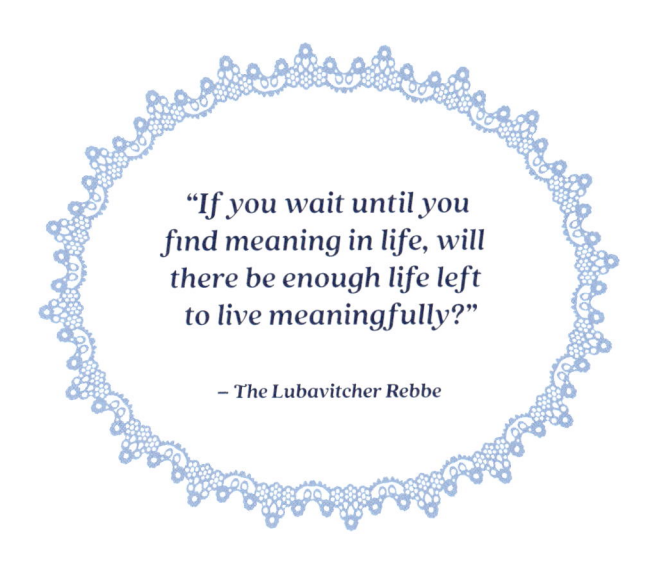

> *"If you wait until you find meaning in life, will there be enough life left to live meaningfully?"*
>
> – The Lubavitcher Rebbe

TAFKID & TALENT

GROWING UP, *TAFKID* WAS ONE OF THOSE SCARY WORDS I didn't want to think about. I shoved *tafkid* into that folder all the way in the far back of my mind, next to *dibbuk* (malicious spirit) and all that horror stuff.

It was only when I was deeply entrenched in doing the work that perks up all my senses, warms my heart, and has my body swaying in sync, that the epiphany started forming. It was only when I was alive in the most vibrant way that everything suddenly clicked.

It was when I was using every one of my talents to share my knowledge with the world. When I finally cleared my throat and let my voice resonate with purpose. When I was in an altered state, so enmeshed with my senses that I could go on and on, without feeling hunger, fatigue, or squashed toes in tight shoes. It was then that I felt truly alive and aligned with my mission.

It was then that it hit me: my mission was my *tafkid*, and I was already doing it!

And it was then that I realized, hey, it wasn't so scary after all!

The rest of the world whizzes by as I am entrenched in this work that lights my heart on fire. I feel it in every bone—this is what I was created to do. This is what my body was programmed for. This is my *tafkid*!

It's a state of utter clarity. It's magic that happens on its own. It can't be explained on paper. And when I'm asked, "Do you have more hours in your day?" or "How do you do it all?" there's no way to explain it, because it's *Himlishe zachen* (Heavenly stuff). It's not me. It's *siyata d'Shmaya*. If I lied that it was me, there would be no way to explain it. He takes care of it all—from exporting the ideas into my brain to supplying me with the endless amount of energy needed for such an undertaking.

I think it would almost be blasphemous to say that He supplied me with all this capability just to stay in there and get moldy. Talent wasn't given just for you. Talent wasn't granted so when you're in *shidduchim*, people can gush, "She's so talented." Talent also wasn't given just to share with your own children and BFFs. Talent was gifted so you can make an impact and achieve your *tafkid*!

Tafkid isn't scary. It doesn't mean you'll have to travel to outer space to identify UFOs up close or to Rwanda to save gorillas. It can mean you'll continue baking the same babka with the streusel crumbs that you're an expert at, but now you'll bake more, with a note attached.

If you are the queen of the circle and possess a dynamic personality with a passion for communication, you'll continue having vibrant, enthusiastic engagements with others, but you'll broaden your circle and perhaps shift focus to more meaningful discussions. If you are a retired artist who got busy doing the things mothers do, you might have to dust off your gift to start creating meaningful art that will light up the world. If you're curious, you may need to resist the allure of reporting on the soap opera of those intriguing neighbors of yours and invest your curiosity into exploring and comprehending life more deeply, enriching your life and the lives of others.

Tafkid doesn't make life scarier; it makes it richer.

It was only once I learned to truly immerse myself in my work that I realized my talent is my *tafkid*. And I realized I had been misled. I felt deceived.

That's why I come to you now, consumed by the intense fire of one who has been deceived, driven by an urgent need to reveal the truth and correct the distortions. *Tafkid* isn't as daunting as they make it seem. Yes, everyone has a *tafkid*, but it's not an intimidating or unknowable concept. Figuring it out isn't the greatest mystery to mankind. Hashem has laid out plenty of clues for you. All you need to do is use your talents and follow your heart. That's really all there is to it.

I'm not trying to oversimplify it, but the opposite approach has done us no good—quite the opposite. Turning *tafkid* into this monster has led many people to believe they can't ever know their purpose in this world, so they don't even try.

"Why are you here?" They shrug, lift their hands. "Who knows?"

That's giving up. That's giving up on life.

And it's disrespectful. We are living in G-d's world. He created the world and us in it because He wants something from us. The ultimate question we should keep asking ourselves should be, "What does the Creator who created me want from me?" When I realize that I am in someone else's world, introspection is due. What am I supposed to do? Am I behaving correctly or incorrectly? Why am I here?

Another way people refer to *tafkid* is with the word *shlichus*. In Chabad *chassidus*, the Alter Rebbe taught that every Jew arrives in this world as G-d's *shaliach*, His personal emissary. *Shlichus* literally means mission—a person is dispatched on a mission, reminding us that we are G-d's messengers here.

The concept of *shlichus* underscores the importance of utilizing our unique gifts and spreading Jewish knowledge, practices, and values to all. We were not sent here solely to dress our children in pretty clothing and capture beautiful pictures. Scrolling through Instagram or discussing trivial matters in the park does not fulfill our *shlichus*.

Each of us has a specific mission. Being a *shliach* is more than just a task; it defines our character and identity.

I didn't say *tafkid* was easy. It's challenging and draining, yet it also fills you up in the most satisfying way. Did you catch that? I know it sounds like an oxymoron, but it's not. If you understand it—good for you! If not, I hope and pray that you will experience it soon, because that's what we were created to do and feel.

The *Chovos Halevavos* urges us to find our strengths and use them, because Hashem gave you those strengths to use for yourself and for others. Any talent a person was given must be used as a tool of influence.

One of the things that has always fascinated me about humanity, and the wonders of the way Hashem created us humans, is how He placed all the answers within us. Our gut feeling, for example—sometimes I feel like that little voice inside of me is almost a form of *ruach hakodesh* (divine inspiration). Hashem created us preloaded with all the answers we need within ourselves.

I always feel an overwhelming rush of *mah rabu ma'asecha Hashem* (how wonderous are Your creations, Hashem) while hiking through the Alps, but I feel an even stronger rush of awe during a cranial sacral therapy session, when the therapist magically identifies the causes of all my stress. I'm constantly amazed by Hashem's creation of these intricate, invisible waves of energy. Energy work remains a mystery to me, yet it never fails to leave me astounded. How does a cranial sacral therapist glean insights about my daughter through me? Within every human body resides a universe of knowledge; within a mother lies the truths and needs of her daughter. It's moments like these that make me marvel at Hashem's intricate design of the world!

We have all the answers inside us, and while we like to learn from others and seek guidance from wiser individuals, we also know that a good coach doesn't tell you what to do or make decisions for you. A good coach asks the right questions that help you find the answers within yourself, so you can make your own decisions based on that. A truly good coach clears the fog so you can come to your own conclusions. She doesn't keep you dependent forever; she teaches and empowers you to coach yourself, to be independent, and to soar—because all the answers are already within you.

Our *tafkid* isn't scary, because we were created fully equipped with all the energy, supplies, and know-how for it. Growing up, I used to think that fulfilling our *tafkid* was a frighteningly difficult task—but it's actually the thing that comes most naturally. It's what you are comfortable doing. It's innate. It's what you excel at. It's about harnessing your talents and embracing them fully.

We enter this world with a specific personal destiny. We each have a task to fulfill, a calling to pursue, and a self to develop. Hashem, our Maker, has endowed us with gifts, talents, passions, and experiences that are unique to each of us—for a reason.

In an episode featuring one of my favorite humans on this planet, Mushky Yiftach, affectionately known as "the duct tape lady," shared the perfect analogy. Mushky explained how a person who isn't scared or grossed out by blood might be suited to be a surgeon. Most people couldn't imagine performing surgery, but for someone who feels fascinated and passionate about it, who dreams of undergoing intensive medical training—this could very well be their clue that their *tafkid* is saving lives.

(I highly recommend watching the episode "Crafting Your Way to Confidence" if you haven't already; it's truly enlightening. And once you're captivated by Mushky, delve into "B'zechus Nashim Tzidkaniyos" for a delightful and entertaining spiel.)

The first step is to use our talents. However, if we use our knack for numbers just to keep our own books organized, or our culinary skills solely to cook the best beef bourguignon for ourselves, or if we paint a stunning picture only for our office wall, we missed the mark.

Purpose is fundamentally about making a difference in the lives of others. We cannot truly live our life's purpose unless we are serving others in some way. Our task in this lifetime isn't to mold ourselves into an ideal that we imagine we should be, but to discover who we already are and to fully embody that, while impacting the world in the most meaningful way possible.

Joy isn't only about fleeting moments of happiness triggered by life's events. Sure, that bite of chocolate can bring a momentary smile—so go ahead and savor it. But true, deeper joy stems from inner peace, love, and the assurance that you're living the life you're meant to lead.

You can accumulate all the small joys your heart desires, but if you find yourself dragging out of bed each morning to a job you dislike or counting down the minutes until you can put your little ones to sleep, just so you can finally relax on the couch and scroll on your phone until your fingers are numb and tingling, you won't feel fulfilled or successful.

Joy is found in living your *tafkid*.

Resistance Is Real

Deep down, we all sense the person we truly are in our hearts.

But many fear uncovering the truth that we are more than what is evident at the surface level. We fear that if we do, things will get complicated. So we push away that small voice that tells us about the capabilities we possess. We ignore our gut instincts and stifle our brilliance. Because once we acknowledge all that we are truly capable of, we fear we'll be obligated to act upon it!

We create all these excuses and made-up *shitas* (positions) and *hashkafos* (worldviews) in our minds. We convince ourselves that if we embrace our ideals, we must prove ourselves worthy of them. We worry about what will become of us. We may lose friends, maybe even family, because they will no longer recognize us. We fear we will end up alone, cast out into the cold.

Of course, this fear is valid, as it often reflects reality. But here's the twist: When we embody who we were meant to be, we find ourselves in new territory—yet not alone. We become an unquenchable, inexhaustible source of wisdom, consciousness, and companionship. Yes, we may lose friends, but we also discover new ones in unexpected places. These are better, truer friends because we are being true to ourselves and, in turn, to them. (For more insights, explore the "Friendships and Friend-Shifts" chapter of this book.)

Even once we discard the excuses and confront the truth, realizing we have the capacity for a bigger life, we often just conjure up more reasons why it can't happen. These excuses come effortlessly—they're instinctive. We inherently fear embracing our true selves because if it's true, we risk becoming estranged from all we know.

There's a plethora of generic excuses fueled by resistance: "I'm the shy type," "I'm not a professional," "Who do you think you are?," "I'm not a Rebbetzin," "I'm not a *mashpia* (spiritual guide)," "It's not *tznius*," fear of failure, concerns about the *mosdos* (educational institutions), the list goes on and on, like the endless line at the DMV on a Friday afternoon.

But the excuse that kept me stuck on this chapter for almost a year was the most popular one among us women, and also in its way the most controversial: "I'm a *Yiddishe mamme*, and my children need me."

I kept playing devil's advocate with myself, driving myself bananas. Eventually, I wrote a letter and sent similar versions to a few respected rabbis, discussing it with them.

Here's the letter I sent to Rabbi Manis Friedman:

> To Rabbi Manis Friedman,
>
> First, I would like to express my heartfelt gratitude for the profound insights and wisdom you have shared through your *shiurim* and YouTube videos. I'm aware that you receive many emails and questions, and I'm concerned that mine might get lost in the shuffle. Nevertheless, I hope you'll take a moment to respond, as my inquiry isn't just a personal one. Given my position of influence, achieving clarity in this area would not only benefit me, but also the broader *klal*.
>
> I'm currently working on another book for women on the topic of "becoming more." My aim is to reach the typical *heimishe* woman and guide her in "Breaking the Yenta Mold" and embracing dignity through infusing her life with meaning, self-reflection, and growth. This book includes chapters on

friendship, personal growth, and the concept of *tafkid* (also known as *shlichus*).

I personally draw immense inspiration from the Lubavitcher Rebbe, particularly from his *sichos* and letters, where he consistently encouraged both women and men to *do more* and make an impact on this world.

A question that constantly plagues me, however, is this: Can having children and motherhood be someone's sole *shlichus* in this world? Are women who only do mothering and homemaking being ignorant or complacent, or are they genuinely focused and invested in their purpose? I'm not asking to pass judgment but to seek understanding, as this concept confuses me. There are conflicting messages regarding women and *shlichus*, and it's perplexing.

Following the Chabad school of thought, which resonates with me deeply, I understand that a person should be a *mashpia*. This calling opens the door to make an impact on the world, or at least influence the people within your reach. However, coming from my Belz upbringing, the way I understood it ... the notion of being a *mashpia* for a woman means being a source of influence for her children and for the gefilte fish cooking in her pot.

Sometimes I wonder: Could it be that motherhood is my ultimate *shlichus*? While mothering is the most precious part of my life, I am convinced it's not my sole purpose in this world. I strongly believe that I have been blessed with many capabilities and potential, and it would be selfish and wasteful to confine them solely to my family and me.

I believe that everyone possesses unique talents that must be put to use. However, is it essential for these talents to serve a larger audience, or is dedicating them to your children sufficient?

When we read the *Chovos Halevavos*, which encourages individuals to find their strengths and employ them as tools for influence, it can be interpreted in two ways:

Mindset #1: If I know how to cook, I can use that skill to prepare delicious meals for Shabbos, for my husband and children. Then I'm using my strengths for good, right?

Mindset #2: Expanding on #1, I can use my cooking skills at home, plus cook for the poor, teach other women how to cook to improve their *shalom bayis* or enhance their *oneg Shabbos*, train others to learn to cook so they can earn a living, and so on.

The first mindset is certainly valid and often where people start, including me. However, staying in this mindset seems complacent to me. Some may argue, "Not everyone is like you," or "Not everyone is capable." There is a prevailing notion that women should focus solely on their homes and avoid additional burdens. In my experience, doing more does not take away; it provides more. As the saying goes, "If you want something done, give it to a busy person." Moreover, I recently heard that the profound satisfaction and the good feeling we experience when doing good is the reward that Hashem bestows upon us when we fulfill our calling. This fulfillment nourishes our *nefesh* because it is an essential aspect of our existence. (I believe this is based on one of the Chazon Ish's letters.) Additionally, when you know that you are meant to do more, you find ways to make it work—because you must.

I firmly believe in empowering women within their own homes. This is where my career began: sharing recipes and tips for homemakers. I have authored two cookbooks with delicious recipes for Shabbos. To me, the home and family are the foundation. Mastering that is essential, but it should also serve as a stepping stone. Perhaps we were placed on this earth to do more than just stay within our *daled amos* (personal domain).

What is the right message to inspire women? Should I encourage them to expand their horizons, empower them to live more fulfilling lives, and stretch themselves beyond their comfort zones? Or should I stick to providing practical tips and recipes for their families?

I hope you can offer some clarity, especially since I am currently writing on this topic.

Rabbi Friedman's secretary responded, and I booked a session with the Rabbi.

Rabbi Friedman began with a statement. "Every talent that Hashem gives needs to be used. Time that Hashem gives needs to be used."

Then he asked, "What is your *daled amos*? Your neighbor next door is not in your *daled amos*? People who want to hear from you are not in your daled amos? There is no question that being a nurturer is not limited to your own children."

In fact, Rabbi Friedman pointed out, "Sara Imeinu was *megayer* the *nashim* (taught the women about G-d)." He also pointed out that, "Just from looking around, you can see that people who have talent and don't use it start to deteriorate."

"How do you know? What are the red flags that you are deteriorating?" I asked.

"If you are feeling resentful, restricted, or you're getting bored making all the kugels. Boredom is the worst thing," he said in his slow, deliberate tone.

"But Rabbi, many people claim that if a woman is running to do other *chessed*, it will take away from her main purpose, from her family…"

"Well, if she's running away *from* her family, that's not kosher. But if a woman is successful with her family, she's got to expand her borders and expand her success. Not by abandoning the family."

I thought to myself, "Wow, that's profound. That's undeniable truth."

But I didn't stop there; this was my chance to lay all my cards on the table. It was an opportunity to clarify all the conflicting messages I had encountered too many times—from society, from the system, and from my own inner tumultuous thoughts (AKA the *yetzer hara*).

I challenged him with the "*hinei ba'ohel*" mantra that I grew up with. That's what they told us every time they wanted to keep women within their frame. I explained that I understood that a woman is meant to stay within the walls of her own home, as the Torah says, "*Hinei ba'ohel*, Sarah was in her tent."

"That's not a *hashkafah*, that's just a bad habit," he said. Remember—Sarah was *megayer* the *nashim*. "The greatest women in history were the businesspeople. They handled the family business, they made all the money, they were working in the market, in the *yerid*. There's no tradition that women have to stay home.

"Adam named his wife Chava," he continued, "because she was *eim kol chai*, the mother of all life. Not just the mother of her own children. All life. All energy. All goodness. Because life and *tov*, good, are synonyms. All life comes from a woman.

"It seems to me that staying home is perhaps a *minhag* (custom), and doing outreach and *tzedakah* (charity) with other Jews is a *chiyuv* (obligation). It's a mitzvah of *ahavas Yisrael*; It's a mitzvah of *chinuch*. It's a mitzvah.

"*Chinuch* isn't just for your own children. If you're *mechanech* other children, it's as if you gave birth to them. It's certainly a mitzvah of *ahavas Yisrael* (love of the Jewish people) and falls under the category of *tzedakah*."

Rabbi Manis Friedman told me that what I was doing was a very big mitzvah. "This could even be *pikuach nefesh* (lifesaving)."

Pikuach nefesh? I was astounded.

"Yes, save marriages, save lives. It's amazing. This confusion is way too painful."

When I hung up the phone, I felt an overwhelming sense of clarity and enlightenment—and I hope I've managed to pass that clarity on to all of you.

Even now, as I recall our conversation, goosebumps cover my arms, and I feel a slight shiver.

The Rebbe spoke extensively about each person being brought into the world to fulfill a *shlichus*, a specific mission. For us women, our paramount *shlichus* consists of being the *akeres habayis* (the mainstay and anchor of our homes), but it doesn't stop there. As is well known, the Rebbe fully believed in a woman's power to anchor our communities and institutions.

As I read in the book *Holy Intimacy* by Sara Morozow and Rivkah Slonim, "You might say the Rebbe fully believed we were superwomen, possessed of infinite powers because we carried infinity within us. He urged us to believe in ourselves and not underestimate our capacities, to firmly anchor ourselves to the *Ein Sof*, the endless energy of Hashem, and expand ourselves to receive the blessings and the light."

In the book, they share a beautiful example in a story related by Batsheva Deren. Her mother-in-law, Kenny Deren *a"h*, was the principal of the Yeshiva Schools Girls High School in Pittsburgh. At a certain point, after suffering a setback in her health, Kenny Deren notified the Rebbe that she planned to promote her daughter-in-law, Batsheva, to the position of principal, while she would continue as a teacher. The Rebbe gave his blessing and consent.

Yet Batsheva was perturbed. At that point she was a mother of seven young children, and was unsure how she would manage to successfully fulfill these seemingly conflicting responsibilities. She wrote to the Rebbe with her concerns and received the following reply:

"Hashem is the Master of power and ability; He has no constraints, and His blessings are of immense proportions. The more you do, the more you will receive." (Translated from *Lashon Hakodesh*.)

Batsheva has kept a copy of this reply in both her school office and at home, as a constant reminder that when one takes care of Hashem's children, we access higher and deeper energy from Hashem's boundless treasure.

On another occasion, I delved into this topic during a session with Rabbi Manis's son, Rabbi Yossi Friedman, a *shliach* in Alabama. He shares his father's profound wisdom and speaks with similar conviction. I gleaned invaluable insights from our hour-long conversation.

"*Chessed* begins at home, but it doesn't end there. Each person can do more. Don't sell yourself short," he emphasized.

The Talmud teaches us that the stork, known in Hebrew as *chassidah*, derives its name from the word for kindness (*chessed*) because it acts kindly towards its companions, mate, and offspring. Since the *chassidah* bird seems to embody the desirable trait of *chessed*, why isn't it kosher?

The Talmud explains that this bird does *chessed* by giving food to its friends. The Chidushei HaRim explains that the *chassidah's* generosity is limited to its own circle of friends, to the exclusion of others. Such partisan kindness is not what the Torah wishes us to practice.

> *Rabbi Adin Even-Yisrael Steinsaltz, a Lubavitcher Chassid and world-renowned Jewish scholar, embarked on a colossal project in 1965 to translate the entire Talmud into modern Hebrew. This undertaking spanned 45 years, culminating in its completion in 2010. His comprehensive translation and commentary have made the Talmud more accessible to a broader audience through clear language and insightful explanations. Known as the Steinsaltz Talmud, his edition includes Hebrew and English translations, along with elucidations and commentaries that help readers grasp the text's complexities. Rabbi Steinsaltz's work has revitalized Talmud study and made Jewish texts more approachable for learners worldwide.*
>
> *The Rebbe supported and backed his work. But at one point, the work seemed too grueling and overwhelming. Rabbi Steinsaltz wrote the Rebbe, "I'm just overwhelmed by work ... I'm involved in three major projects and dozens of smaller ones ... It's overwhelming!" He wanted to know, "What should I drop?" Each project was important on a different level and in a different way, but it seemed to be too much for one person.*
>
> *The main point of the answer he received from the Rebbe was: "You go on. You continue to do all these things. And try to do more things." That was the last message he heard from the Rebbe.*

But I Don't Have Talent!

"I'm not talented." "I have two left hands."

There's no such thing! The idea that talent is some magical gift only a few are born with is a myth that holds many of us back. Talent isn't about being perfect from the start; it's about finding what you love, working at it, and letting yourself grow. When we call ourselves untalented, we miss out on the joy of learning and the thrill of improvement.

First, an important disclaimer: a big mistake is that people often associate being talented with the arts, such as drawing, music, and dance. But talent isn't restricted to what you would perform at a talent show. You can be amazingly talented in so many different ways. For instance, some people have a natural gift for problem-solving, which makes them excellent engineers or scientists. Others might have a talent for empathy and communication, making them wonderful therapists or teachers. There are those who excel at organizing and planning, which is crucial for successful event coordinators or project managers. Even talents like cooking, gardening, or being great at listening and supporting friends are incredibly valuable. Talent is diverse and unique to each individual, and it encompasses far more than what we typically see on stage.

Unfortunately, people with low self-esteem often feel so disconnected that they don't recognize their true strengths. Fortunately, it's not the greatest mystery, because the things we're good at are often what we enjoy doing the most. Projects we find pleasure in at work, hobbies we carve out time for, or dreams we harbor are good indicators of our talents.

If you're feeling stuck, follow these steps to discover your hidden talents:

1. *Find Your Curiosity*
   Identify current interests. Make a mental note of the activities you currently enjoy or used to enjoy when you allowed yourself time to indulge in what you loved. Ask yourself specifically what inspires and satisfies you about these activities. Assess your interests and skills. Find ways to engage in these activities more often.

2. *Ask Others About Your Strengths*
   Engage in conversations with friends, family, and colleagues who know you well. They may have observations about your strengths and talents that you haven't considered. Often, others can perceive abilities in you that you may not recognize as special because they come naturally and effortlessly. Their perspectives can provide valuable insight, and help you identify your special *kochos* that you may not have acknowledged before.

3. Ask Others About their Interests
Talk to friends, family, and colleagues about how they discovered their passions.

4. Reflect on Childhood
Think back to your childhood interests and activities. Often, our childhood passions provide clues to our innate talents and preferences. Revisiting these can spark new ideas and insights into what truly resonates with you.

5. Change Your Beliefs
If you're feeling stuck and untalented, remember it's often all in your mind! And that's where the first needle of change must move.

A *fixed mindset* is focused on talent. Those with a fixed mindset believe statements like, "You are smart, so you will do well in life," and, "You are naturally gifted, and that will take you far." They categorize people based on natural abilities and believe that factors like IQ, GPA, and SAT scores define intelligence and limit potential. When your potential is measured against a fixed criteria, falling short can make you doubt your own intelligence and value.

I was a failing student. I never earned a high school diploma, let alone attended seminary or college. I tried retaking a few tests, got engaged, and gave up. If I had let that define my potential, I would never be writing this book—my third as of this writing.

When we let grades or performance reviews limit our potential, it affects our belief in what we can achieve. The fixed mindset might not bother you when life is sailing along smoothly and you're succeeding at everything. But when struggles or failures hit, the fixed mindset can crush your hope for the future.

A *growth mindset* is what we should strive to achieve. It opens doors to incredible possibilities. Those with a growth mindset believe that through effort, they can learn new things, improve personality traits, and even increase intelligence. They are resilient in the face of failure and see natural traits as starting points rather than limitations. A growth mindset believes in continuous growth through experience, embracing change, and evolving substantially through actions. Unlike a fixed mindset, a growth mindset thrives on effort!

My Mission

With *Inspired Living*, I embarked on a journey that pushed me far beyond my comfort zone. One after the next, I met incredible women who were essentially strangers, and I didn't just chit-chat, but was vulnerable. Filming a deep conversation with another woman is a highly intimate experience; looking into their eyes for two hours straight and coming at them with my curiosity and deep questions is daunting. It's a privilege to connect with so many diverse, awesome ladies, and I feel fortunate to facilitate these conversations and be the *shliach* to share their wisdom with the world.

I'm passionate about addressing the real emotional struggles we women face daily. I wish more women would discuss and share coping skills as freely as they discuss their recipes and their children's preferences. Knowing how to whip up a delicious Shabbos meal is important, but it's not what will make you the best mother or wife. Emotional knowledge and mindset shifts are crucial to go from surviving to thriving. My goal with *Inspired Living* was to fill that void.

I believe we women need inspirational and supportive messages that shift our mindsets and empower us in relatable, practical ways. For so many, hearing this kind of basic, crucial talk usually means paying $250 an hour for a coach or therapist. Many women don't have the amazing friends that I do (yet!) to act as their free therapists, to enlighten and support them. They might gossip and discuss surface-level topics but avoid delving into their real challenges—because they don't know how. With *Inspired Living*, I wanted to open the conversation and demonstrate a different way of connecting.

Hosting and creating these conversations revealed that I'm not alone in my frame of mind. I discovered thousands of women who share my passion for down-to-earth talk and shifting negative, complaining conversations to a calmer, more empowering way of discussing a topic. The *Inspired Living* platform became a haven crafted exclusively for women who seek more from life!

The Rebbe said, "When we look at the world and only see a problem, it's us who have the problem. But when we look at the world and see a solution, it means this is the corner of the world we're meant to light up." When you connect deeply with others, it elevates what you are already doing to the next level. It's what makes life exhilarating and deeply fulfilling.

Learning and keeping our minds intellectually stimulated is essential for many reasons. It's important for our sanity, focus, self-growth, and our marriages. It's crucial to have interesting topics to discuss with your husband, beyond the neighbors and the children and things floating around the house. My mission was to bring these vital conversations in a digestible format to the average woman in a way that feels like entertainment, not a preachy *shiur*.

I want women to come for the entertainment, tips, and recipes and, as they watch, feel their minds opening and expanding, like a flower blossoming in the sunlight. I want them to experience the exhilarating sensation of their intelligence growing, feeling smarter and more capable with each moment. I want them to revel in the joy of learning. Because once they feel this, they are welcomed into a new, exhilarating way of life—a warm, vibrant life filled with endless meaning and deep fulfillment.

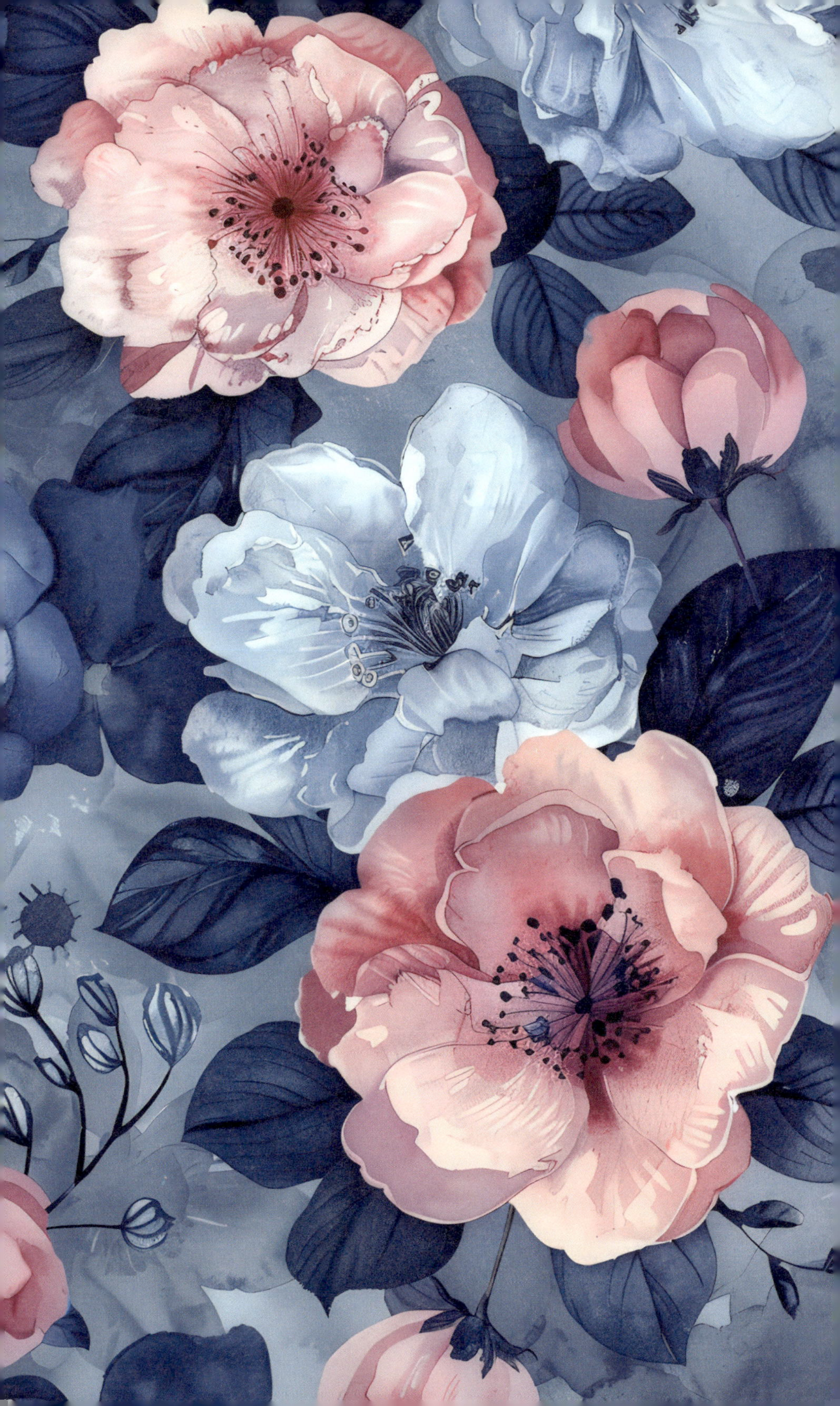

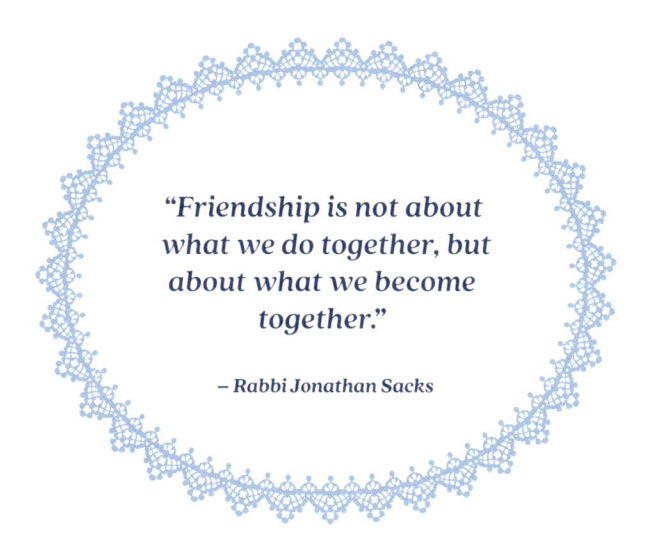

> *"Friendship is not about what we do together, but about what we become together."*
>
> – Rabbi Jonathan Sacks

FRIENDSHIPS & FRIEND-SHIFTS

"**SHE DOESN'T *FARGIN* YOU!**"

This was my husband's response when I recounted a comment from a friend. His words were like a sharp knife, slicing through the delicate threads of our friendship and exposing imperfections that I didn't want to face.

I lashed out in defense. "Don't talk like that about my friends!"

"But she's not a real friend. Don't you see?"

Ouch.

It wasn't the first time he had spoken his mind. Each time, it felt as though he was disregarding my feelings with a lack of thoughtfulness. I was down on my hands and knees, tirelessly attempting to keep this friendship standing, even as the pieces stubbornly resisted alignment and threatened to topple over. If I listened to him, it could all fall apart.

It didn't matter how imperfect this relationship was. To me, it was better than nothing. His unsolicited blunt comments were unwelcome, regardless of their accuracy. They felt hurtful, like a careless toddler crawling mindlessly right into my carefully constructed tower.

It got me mad each time, and I made sure he knew it.

"What do you want from me?" I snapped, my voice tinged with desperation. "You want me to be friendless?"

That's how I was back then. I held on to friends who envied me, didn't serve me, did nothing but bring me down. I tiptoed around them, trying my best to keep them happy even though they didn't do the same for me.

I vividly remember the early days of my career, when one of my friends envied me for the most ridiculous things, like getting free food at restaurants. I would go out with her, treat her, pamper her. Give her a piece of it, so she felt she was gaining from my success and share in my joy.

I put on a pretty show, measured my words.

Deep down, I knew this wasn't how things should be, but I convinced myself that I wasn't being ignorant or stupid. I was just being cautious so I wouldn't end up friendless. Yes, the fear of being friendless was a real, palpable terror that loomed over me every day.

I wasn't nearly as accomplished then as I am today, but I was still consumed with thoughts of how to compensate my friends for my achievements. I was determined not to outshine them or make them feel uncomfortable. Looking back, it's almost comical how much effort I put into camouflaging my success in bubble wrap before being with them. But in the moment, it felt necessary: the only way to preserve our friendship.

It was back when my business model was different. I had a boutique-style marketing firm with a cute little team, and we primarily focused on marketing for various companies—branding, advertising, social media management, and events. I had just landed a major account that was keeping me very busy. Naturally, I confided in my friend about feeling overwhelmed. She seemed not to understand the reason I was, in her words, "driving myself crazy," asking why I took on the account if it was so much work. I didn't understand what she didn't get.

You see, my husband and I had just moved to Lakewood and had purchased a small starter home. It was a great deal, but we had borrowed a lot of money for the down payment and moving expenses. I was just being responsible. Because let's face it, money doesn't grow on trees. And that's why I was working hard to pay it all back as soon as possible.

Incidentally, I'm grateful that I pushed myself to overwork when I was younger with a smaller family and had the stamina for it. My husband and I worked tirelessly for several years, and with Hashem's help, we were able to pay off our debts and secure a roof over our heads.

I explained to her that it was worth it financially and that the client was paying a significant amount. My friend wouldn't let up. She kept trying to guess how much they were paying. I didn't disclose the exact amount; I knew she would envy me and assume I was rolling in dough, even though the money was intended to pay off our debt. She persistently made jokes about my supposed wealth, insinuating that I should keep footing the bill when we were out together, since she had decided I was making $10,000 a month.

She continued this banter during our girls' nights out, whether we were out for fun or dinner. Each time she joked, "You can afford this, you're making $10,000 anyway..." I felt increasingly uncomfortable. Her remarks made me uneasy, and I didn't know how to handle the sense of privilege she imposed on me. I felt lost and unable to silence her, so I swiped my card, paid like a *mammele* and laughed it off with a wave of my hand. Occasionally I paid for her drink, her ticket or her portion. I could afford it, I reasoned. And a friendship was worth way more than a $30 portion.

Of course, I knew that wasn't the ideal situation. It didn't feel good. I felt taken advantage of. She somehow made me feel guilty for my success. Friends should be happy for each other, not envious. But at the time, I didn't know what that looked like. I was constantly trying to hide my success and shrink myself so as not to make my friend uncomfortable. It was a miserable way to live, but I didn't know any better.

These days, when I achieve success, my friends are genuinely happy for me. I no longer feel the need to shrink my success, hide, or do things I hadn't planned. I no longer fear their envy. Deep in my heart, I hear their joyous and proud voices celebrating my every accomplishment.

They even buy me gifts and send me cards. They take me out to celebrate. Can you believe it?

It's a beautiful thing. I never dreamed that such goodness, selflessness, and genuine happiness could exist between friends. I never knew that women could celebrate each other's successes, even when they're not experiencing their own. I never even dared to wish for it, because I didn't know it existed. It's amazing how shared joy can bring people together and make life so much richer and fulfilling.

What's ironic is that despite all of my efforts toward keeping these so-called friends back then, they all left me at one point or another. One by one, each friend ended it at a different time, each with a different rhyme and reason. Every time it happened it felt like a fresh wound. One moment they were there, and the next, they gave me the coldest of shoulders.

I remember one friend in particular who left me standing outside in the pouring rain. It wasn't until later that I found out she was pregnant, and I tried to be *dan l'kaf zechus* (judge her favorably), blaming it on her hormones. But even after the baby was born and she recuperated from the birth, she never made up or apologized for her hurtful actions.

There was another friend who left me after a misunderstanding. I poured my heart out in countless messages, apologizing for my mistake and hoping for reconciliation. As we say in Yiddish, "*Ich hub meech oisgeteen naket far her*, I got undressed naked for her." It's not the most pleasant expression, but it perfectly captures the depth of my devotion—how I was willing to do anything for her, even if it meant compromising my own dignity. But it was like trying to catch a bar of soap in a bathtub; she kept slipping away, leaving me questioning what I could have done differently.

I still remember the sting of each ignored message, pouring my heart out to a friend who had already checked out. "Please forgive me. I'm so sorry," I wrote, begging for another chance. But the response I received was cold and distant, lacking any warmth or empathy. She said she forgave me, but her actions spoke louder than her words. It was clear she didn't believe me, didn't like me—was no longer interested in me.

I can still feel the desperation of those moments, down on my knees, pleading with my last remaining friends to stick around so I wouldn't be left alone. Despite my best efforts, the understanding and support I craved never came. Instead, I was left feeling foolish for each apology I sent.

What is Friendship?

"We're friends, so give me a discount."

"We're friends, so send me pictures of your family."

Are we really friends? What truly defines friendship? People often toss the word around lightly, and sometimes I wonder if they even understand its meaning. I mean, for a long time, I know I didn't.

The existence of good friends is a treasure that's hard to come by. Not every person who chills with you, shops with you, or provides entertainment qualifies as a real friend. Entertainment is something you can buy with money, but a *kesher nafshi*, a soul connection, is invaluable.

Real friends are not about benefits or perks. I have friends who don't do me daily favors. I'm not sending them my children when I go on vacation. They live far away. Yet they are always there for me. They understand me on a deeper level. It's a connection that defies description. They've heard me at my lowest, held space for my deepest pain, and have never judged me. Even if they don't know half of what's happening, I know they understand me.

Friendship is a delicate and vital topic, particularly for us women. There is so much talk and so many tips out there on *chinuch*, homemaking, and marriage, but our friendships are an overlooked aspect of our lives. We tend to underestimate its significance, even though it profoundly shapes and influences our sense of being. And just as with any other relationship, our friendships require effort, nurturing, and attention.

We need to cultivate awareness and understanding to know what is right and wrong in our interactions with our friends. We need guidance and tips to help us navigate the ups and downs of these relationships.

Yet society often overlooks the importance of friendship, treating it as a luxury rather than a vital aspect of our lives. It's as if we're saying, "Who needs friends when you have a pile of laundry to fold?" We treat friendship as if it's an unnecessary, optional add-on to life, like those tomato holders or banana slicers designed specifically for cutting bananas into even slices.

But let's face it: we can't survive without our friends.

As we grow and evolve, we go through a myriad of experiences with our friends. When we feel let down or betrayed by those we trust, the pain can be unbearable, searing through our souls like hot embers. And when they drop us altogether, it can feel like a sudden and painful divorce, leaving us reeling and disoriented.

I know firsthand the agony of losing close friends. It took me months to come to terms with the fact that some of the people I had considered my closest allies were no longer there for me. I also know that I am not alone in this experience. The bonds of friendship run deep, and when they are severed, the hurt can be profound.

Friendship is one of the key factors that determine our self-growth or lack thereof. They say that you can tell a person's character by the company she keeps. By observing the personalities of those in her immediate circle, you can gain an approximate sense of the kind of person she is. If you're serious about your self-growth, you gotta be serious about your friends.

Let's be real, ladies. We've been settling for mediocrity in ourselves and in our friendships for far too long. Yet nothing has the power to fuel us, inspire joy, and help us grow quite like our friendships do. Good friends are like a secret weapon, but we're not using them to our advantage. Why? Because we're afraid to ask for what we really want and need. We're afraid to rock the boat, so we just live with friendships that take more than they give. Come on, ladies, we can do better!

Because we've convinced ourselves that good friendships are a luxury, we let them gather dust on the shelf, like that fancy dress we bought but never wear. We put friendship last on our list (if it's on the list at all). We'll cancel that coffee date or girls' night out if we're overwhelmed with work, family obligations, or a new pregnancy. It just feels unnecessary next to our other responsibilities. But let me tell you, canceling those catch-up calls is costing us more than we realize. Even if we don't see it.

Now, I know it's easy to spot the obvious signs when a friendship is not working. But there are usually clues long before things blow up in our faces. That's why self-awareness and being true to yourself are so important. You need to be your own best friend first, so you can listen to those nagging feelings and anxieties that start as a whisper but only get louder if you ignore them.

Want to know if your friends are right for you? Start by paying attention to how you feel when you interact with certain people. That's the first step to awareness.

Do you feel at ease? Anxious? Guilty? Uplifted?

Do you feel like yourself?

Next time you see a certain friend's number pop up on your screen and *s'vert deech shvartz faren oigen*, you see black before your eyes—take a step back and make a *cheshbon hanefesh*, a personal accounting. Are you taking care of yourself? Are you attuned to your own needs? The more you ignore those feelings, the bigger they'll grow, and the worse the relationship will be for both of you.

Let's stop treating our friendships like an afterthought, ladies. They're the secret sauce to a happy and fulfilling life. I am filled with gratitude for my friends who have been a constant source of support in my life. They are the ones who help me become a better person, both in the big decisions I make as a public figure, and in the small things that happen every day in the chaos of family life.

Growing Through Friendship

The other day a friend texted me: "Listening to Mr. X featured on this podcast, pretty interesting." I had seen it featured, but I wasn't attracted to it. In fact, I replied, "Really? I would never think of clicking on that. I don't know why I'm not attracted to him. He seems like a big shot..."

You see, I'm not a perfect human being—shocker, I know! I can be guilty of judging and gossiping, just like any other flawed creature roaming this planet. But this is where my amazing friends save me. They lift me up, they challenge me, and they make me want to be a better person. They are constantly growing and changing.

My friend's response to my dismissive text was incredible. She said, "I had a really bad outlook on him as well, and it was worth it to get rid of that. It's interesting, he had a difficult life."

These are the friends I truly respect. They are always seeking growth and self-improvement, and they inspire those around them to do the same. Their positivity and willingness to learn and change is contagious, and I feel incredibly lucky to have them in my life.

After listening to my friend's insights, I realized that I had been quick to judge, and that there was much more to this person than I had originally thought. And guess what? I listened to the podcast, and my perspective on another *Yid* completely changed. It was a small moment, but it left me feeling like a better person!

A friend will meet you for coffee, listen to your problems and keep you company, but a really good friend will also encourage you to grow, nudging you without preaching to become a better person. Good people bring up others with them, automatically.

Who needs gossip when you have friends who help you grow? Everyone deserves friends like these—because blossoming feels much better than blabbering about each other!

So often, women bond over shared wounds and problems; they find themselves venting about the same frustrations, and before you know it, they are consistently coming together to commiserate. At first, it can feel validating to find solace in the shared experience. However, over time, it can become pretty toxic and hinder your self-growth. You don't want to remain stuck marinating in the mud all day. You want to be around women who are eager to rise, shake it off, move on at one point, and step onto solid ground. While sharing and validating each other is essential, we must consider at the end of the day: is this relationship and these conversations lifting us up or dragging us down?

Now, I get it. Sometimes it's tempting to bond with someone over a shared enemy or a frustrating situation. But if that's all you're doing, it's not a healthy or sustainable friendship. Negativity can seep into your subconscious and affect your overall wellbeing. Let's aim for positive and uplifting friendships that make us feel good about ourselves and our lives. Friends that vent about their joy, too. Not just their problems!

Ask yourself: Who are you with when you're feeling your best?

Now let's talk *tachlis*! I'll try to help you out with some concrete tips and lists. I'm such a list person, I have lists for my lists, and even lists for the lists that I haven't made yet. I think I need a list of all my lists, just to keep track of them all!

Anyway, where was I? Let me check my list...

Oh yes, don't worry, I've got a list for everything! From spotting those red flags to making new friends, I've got your back. So sit tight, or rather sit comfortably, and here we go!

Ending a Friendship

Let's talk red flags, my friend. It's important to recognize when a friendship may not be serving you in a positive way. **Here are some signs to watch out for:**

- When you don't like how you feel when you're with that person.
- When you don't like how you're acting or speaking around her.

- When you feel a sense of dread or negativity when you see her name pop up on your screen.
- When you feel like you're walking on eggshells around her.
- When you feel like you're suppressing parts of yourself to please her.
- When your primary bonding is over negativity, complaining, and gossip.
- When you're often left with a lingering sense of discomfort or unease after conversations with her.

You'll notice that I didn't label this person toxic. To be honest, I cringe when I hear this expression thrown around in today's pop psychology environment. More often than not, people aren't necessarily toxic; they're just not good for *you*. They don't contribute positively to your life, and they may hinder your personal growth or sanity. Often labeling someone as toxic is like blaming the pizza for your stomachache. Sure, the pizza may have contributed, but you also chose to eat three slices, right?

Labelling someone a toxic friend can be dangerous because it shifts the focus away from ourselves. We can't just blame others for everything that goes wrong in our relationships. We need to take responsibility for our own behavior and examine how we may have contributed to the situation.

The other day I saw this amazing quote on a friend's status: "When you persist in being bothered by someone who refuses to change, you also refuse to change."

Read that again.

Before you label someone toxic, consider this: How many times have you ignored your feelings of angst when you're around her? How often have you kept quiet about a friend's repeated behavior that frustrates or upsets you? How many times have you laughed at her mean-spirited jokes, even though they were far from funny?

How many times have you felt misunderstood or unseen by a friend and just swallowed it instead of standing up for yourself? How many times have you compromised yourself, your basic rights, and your self-dignity, in your decision to be the bigger person or out of fear of upsetting her?

Being close to a friend doesn't mean that things will always be easy. Every relationship has its ups and downs, and true friendship can withstand tensions, disagreements, and absences.

However, it's important to recognize when a relationship is not worth the effort and to let it go. This can be especially true for old friendships when it's clear that if you had met that person now, as an adult, you probably would not have formed a close bond with her. It's important to acknowledge these relationships and move on when necessary.

If you want to grow, here's a list of some friends you may want to consider dropping:

- They have a way of making you feel terrible about yourself. You don't feel good about yourself when spending time with them.
- They only reach out when they need or want something from you.
- They frequently belittle or mock you.
- They treat this relationship like a competition and see every interaction as an opportunity to prove they are better than you.
- They aren't happy for you when good things happen to you.
- They are energy-drainers who bring an endless supply of drama into your life.
- They thrive off of drama and gossip and talk nonstop about others behind their backs (which means they probably talk about you behind your back, too).
- They are a bad influence and pressure you to engage in activities that go against your values or comfort level.

Imagine your life without this person—is it a weight off your shoulders?

Listen, it's not always easy to end a friendship, but sometimes it's necessary for your own growth and wellbeing. Here's a brief list outlining the basic steps to take when ending a friendship and shifting the direction of your life:

1. *Process it*
   Before cutting off a friendship, take time to fully process your emotions. Don't act out of anger or hurt.

2. Create a plan

How do you want to end the friendship? Consider whether you need to communicate with the person, or if you can simply cool things off slowly and respectfully. If you've had a long and close relationship with someone, it's important to approach the situation with respect and sensitivity. Even though you may no longer feel the warmth and closeness you once did, it's *mentschlich* to acknowledge the history and positive times you shared together. Having a conversation can bring a sense of closure and allow you both to move on. It's not an easy thing to do, but it's a brave and mature way to handle the situation.

3. Iron out the details

If you do decide to communicate, think about what you want to say and be sensitive to the other person's feelings. Take some time to reflect on it. Do you need to explain in detail why you can't continue the friendship, or is a more general message enough? It's important to weed out any anxieties or excuses you may be making, and communicate gently in a way that is sensitive to her feelings. Whether it's through writing or verbal communication, aim to express yourself clearly and respectfully.

4. Give yourself grace

Give yourself permission to grieve the loss of the friendship, as it can be a painful experience. It's natural to feel a sense of loss and to miss the person you once knew, even if you've realized it hasn't been good for you.

Don't beat yourself up with guilt for choosing the wrong friend. It's what I like to call a "friend-shift"—people who come into our lives to take us to a certain place, but can only take us so far. And remember, the only way you are going to recognize a good friend is if you've had some friendships that were not good for you.

As Jews, we believe that everything happens is for a reason, and we shouldn't cry over spilled milk. Remember that there's a lesson to be learned from every experience, even if it's a painful one. So give yourself the grace to grieve, along with the strength to move on and embrace the new opportunities that come your way.

What Does a True Friendship Look Like?

Let's move on to the good stuff—real friends. The kind of friend who will listen without judgment and who'll tell you when you've got lipstick on your teeth.

What is a true friend?

While no two people are completely alike and there's no such thing as a perfect friendship, there are certain fundamental traits that define a solid and genuine friendship. Here's another handy dandy list:

1. You feel good around each other

In a true friendship, feeling good around each other means being able to share both positive and negative aspects of life without fear of judgment or rejection. Whether you've shared your proudest accomplishments, vented about your frustrations, or revealed your biggest dreams, both friends leave the interaction feeling heard, accepted, and supported. It's the feeling of warmth and comfort that comes from knowing you can be your authentic self around someone without pretense or reservation, and feeling good about yourself when you're with them.

As the great author Maya Angelou once said, "I've learned that people will forget what you said, people will forget what you did, but people will never forget how you made them feel."

2. It works for you

There are chessed cases, and there are real friends. They are both important to have, but they do not fall into the same category. I don't know about you, but I personally don't have the energy for high-maintenance friendships. Friends are where you go to revive yourself after you've spent your last energies on your toddler's tantrums, your teenager's sarcasm, and your *chessed* cases.

A real friend should be smooth and easy. She speaks your language so she can revive you. She isn't someone you have to constantly bend over backwards for. You are able to be honest with each other about what you need and can handle from this relationship.

The other day, my friend from Monsey actually drove all the way to Lakewood to meet me. I can't express how awesome that felt, that she drove all the way to have lunch with me! For years I was doing that for friends who never did it in return.

Ah, the joy of finally reuniting with a dear friend, face-to-face! As we settled into our vinyl seats at the café, our conversation quickly carried us away to the extent that we nearly forgot to place our orders. The ticking clock reminded us of our time constraints, so we reluctantly paused our animated exchange to place our orders, though our minds remained wholly absorbed in our conversation.

Before we knew it, the piping hot food was placed in front of us, delightful aromas and flavors adding to the warmth of our reunion. Our conversation danced effortlessly from topic to topic, each exchange infused with vibrant energy and genuine curiosity.

As we sat together, an hour passed by in the blink of an eye. "Oh well, it was short and sweet," I remarked. And with a heartfelt nod, she echoed, "That's the kind of friends I need."

She didn't require four hours of my time to feel valued; she, like me, had a busy schedule. Her honesty was refreshing. It was liberating that she didn't expect lengthy daily phone calls to maintain our closeness. She voiced her needs, which aligned perfectly with mine. What more could a girl ask for?

That's the kind of open, upfront friendships I wish for every woman!

I've discovered what works best for me, and I've realized that these types of friendships are the ones that truly resonate with me. If my type of communication doesn't work for you, I'm sorry, but perhaps we're not meant to be friends.

I've learned to follow my gut. There are countless individuals with positive energy, and those are the kind of people I want to surround myself with.

It's not easy. Sometimes I meet someone and we hit it off perfectly, enjoying a wonderful camaraderie. But then she starts probing into areas where I simply don't want her to be. At that point I find myself giving her the cold shoulder, making it clear that this dynamic isn't going to work. Regardless of how uncomfortable it is, I remind myself that it's the right thing to do, because my energy is not unlimited. I have to preserve it.

3. *You both make a consistent effort to connect*

Like any relationship, a friendship requires consistent effort and attention to thrive. While it's not necessary to talk every day, it's important to stay somewhat connected and show interest in each other's lives.

If one person is doing all the work to stay in touch, the friendship may become one-sided and unbalanced. It's normal for one friend to require more support during tough times. However, there has to be a level of balance. If you find yourself being the only one reaching out, it's time to reassess the friendship's dynamic. It's not a matter of keeping score or counting texts, but if you're constantly initiating conversations with little reciprocation, then the relationship is not in sync.

If you limit your conversations with a friend to just once a year, chances are you'll end up spending the entire time discussing mundane topics like, "How are the kids?" or "Is your husband still working that job?" Because of that, the friendship may not feel as fulfilling as it could be. If you check in with your friends more regularly, you can bypass all that surface-level chit-chat and dive straight into the more substantial and stimulating stuff.

This is really easy these days, even if you're busy! Platforms like WhatsApp can be very beneficial—they make it easy to tend to friendships and stay updated on a regular basis. You can have more in-depth conversations about the things that matter most to you and build a more meaningful and soulful connection when you finally do get on the phone or meet for coffee. After all, it's the real, heartfelt conversations that truly nourish and deepen our relationships.

You want your friend to reach out to you about spending time together, not just to feel that she's interested in you, but because you often need that gentle nudge to take care of your social needs. If you're busy like me, having someone encourage you to make time for outings can make all the difference. Sometimes you'll be the one making sure an outing happens, but you need that from her too. Amid hectic schedules and natural resistance, spending time together can easily slip through the cracks.

True friends understand and anticipate each other's needs, making the effort to check in and reach out. It's not just about making time for yourself, but for each other. Friends are here to support and uplift us, and that includes making sure we prioritize and cherish the time we spend together.

4. You feel safe to be vulnerable with one another

Building a deep and genuine connection with someone is one of the greatest challenges and rewards of true friendship. No matter how much time you spend together, without vulnerability, the relationship will lack depth.

As the proverb in *Mishlei* (12:25) says, "*Da'agah belev ish, yisuchenu acheirim.* Share your heart with someone else; they'll help you bear the burden."

If you come across someone who constantly keeps her guard up, never admits her mistakes, and refuses to show any weakness, she may not be a true friend. True closeness and connection can only be achieved when we share our common struggles and shortcomings. Only then can the friendship grow and thrive, as both friends support and understand each other on a deeper level.

It takes bravery to open yourself up emotionally, so be selective. Only bare your soul with those who have earned the right to see it.

Establishing meaningful connections and receiving empathy is a delicate process. It's important to be authentic, but not to blindly trust anyone. While there may be many wonderful people in our lives, only a select few can provide the true compassion and understanding needed in our dark moments. Vulnerability with the wrong person can easily backfire. To ensure a solid connection, it's essential to know when it's safe to share our shame or darkness.

Don't be vulnerable with:

- The woman who reacts with wide-eyed fascination to your pain, as if it's a form of sensational entertainment. I call these people yentas. I grew up around too many of them! They tend to focus on the drama of a situation rather than the emotional wellbeing of their friends.

- The woman who can't handle your pain. She hears the story and actually feels uncomfortable or embarrassed for you. She might shift her weight from one foot to another, fidget, or avoid eye contact. She might gasp in horror, making you feel like you have to comfort her, instead of the other way around.

- The woman who offers patronizing sympathy instead of genuine empathy. She says things like, "Oh, you poor thing," and, "Don't worry, everything happens for a reason," rather than offering true empathy that sounds more like, "I get it, I feel with you. I've been there."

- The woman who needs you to be the pillar of worthiness and strength. She can't help because she's too disappointed. You've let her down. She may scold you, "How did you let this happen? What were you thinking?"

- The woman who refuses to acknowledge the seriousness of your situation or emotions.

  "You're exaggerating. It wasn't that bad." Or she invalidates your feelings by saying things like, "You're overreacting" or "It's not a big deal." She may minimize your experience with comments like, "It could be worse."

- The woman who bashes your loved ones. She starts speaking negatively about the person you're complaining about, such as your husband or mother. She crosses boundaries and doesn't respect the importance of these relationships in your life. She doesn't know her place and fails to understand the need for sensitivity towards your loved ones, even when you are temporarily hurt by them.

- The woman who always turns it back to herself. "That's nothing! Listen to what happened to me one time!"

Which brings me to #5:

5. You have confidence in each other
There's a foundation of unconditional confidence that makes it possible to build a deep relationship. You can feel the warmth and sincerity in your heart as you think about your friend. It's clear that you genuinely care about her and want the best for her. That's why sending a message that reads, "Don't tell anyone!" seems unnecessary. You know your friend has your back, and you trust her not to do anything that might compromise your privacy. A good friend should have the intuition to know what you wouldn't want shared with others, and that's what sets her apart from casual acquaintances.

It's important to avoid gossiping with friends, since talking behind other people's backs can erode trust. Gossiping with friends may create a temporary feeling of unity and excitement, but it ultimately doesn't foster genuine friendship. This is because you can assess a friend's trustworthiness by observing how she talks about others. If she shares juicy details with you about mutual friends, it's likely that she's sharing similar details about you with others.

Trust is built through consistent behaviors that demonstrate reliability, honesty, and integrity. These actions include offering genuine empathy, active listening, and consistent support. Honesty and vulnerability are also crucial for building trust, as they create an atmosphere of openness and authenticity. Ultimately, building trust takes time and effort, but it's an essential ingredient for any strong and lasting friendship.

6. You respect each other's boundaries
A true friend will always respect your privacy and personal values, and never push you to do or share something you're uncomfortable with. If she asks you something once and you avoid answering, she will never ask again. The relationship takes priority over any curiosity.

Considerate friends understand that friendships are a two-way street and that both parties need space and time to themselves at certain points. They understand that sometimes you may be unavailable and will respect that without taking it personally or making you feel guilty. This shows that they value your wellbeing and the health of the friendship, rather than their own desires and needs.

They will avoid sensitive topics, check in with you before making assumptions, and apologize and adjust their behavior if they unintentionally cross your boundaries.

7. You have each other's back

Having each other's back includes being honest with each other, which is built on trust. A true friend will give you honest feedback, even when it's difficult to hear, and encourage you to be your best self. This doesn't mean constantly sharing unsolicited opinions, but being willing to provide an honest perspective when asked. A genuine friend will check in first by asking, "Do you want my advice?" or "I have a suggestion that may or may not be helpful. If you are ever interested, let me know and I would be happy to share." She will know how to express her opinion in a warm and gentle way.

8. You can forgive each other

One of the most important aspects of a strong and lasting friendship is the ability to forgive each other. No friendship is perfect, and there will inevitably be disagreements, misunderstandings, or hurt feelings along the way. However, what sets a true friendship apart is the willingness to work through these challenges together, to mend any rifts that may arise, and to ultimately come out stronger on the other side. A friendship that can weather the ups and downs of life, that can bounce back from moments of rupture and repair, is one that will stand the test of time. When you can forgive each other and move forward with compassion and understanding, you show that you don't stand on ceremony, and that you value your relationship more than your pride.

9. You accept each other

A true friend is someone who accepts you for who you are, flaws and all, and doesn't try to change you or make you feel inferior. They celebrate your successes and are genuinely happy for you, without envy or jealousy. A true friendship is like coming home, a place where you can let your guard down and truly belong. It's a sanctuary where you're not judged, where you're accepted for who you are, and where your most authentic self is celebrated.

A true sense of belonging in a friendship is about being accepted for who you truly are, without having to put on a mask or tiptoe around. As Brené Brown beautifully states, "True belonging is the spiritual practice of believing in and belonging to yourself so deeply that you can share your most authentic self with the world and find sacredness in both being a part of something and standing alone in the wilderness. True belonging doesn't require you to change who you are; it requires you to be who you are."

These words are worth framing and hanging where you can always see them.

If you're constantly shrinking yourself or trying to fit in with your friends, it may be a sign that you don't truly belong in that group. And here's Brené's crystal-clear sentence describing the difference between belonging and fitting in: "Belonging is being accepted for you. Fitting in is being accepted for being like everyone else."

Brené adds, "Belonging is being somewhere where you want to be, and they want you. Fitting in is being somewhere where you want to be, but they don't care one way or the other."

Nurturing Friendships

If you're nodding along to all of this, feeling grateful for that amazing friend/friends in your life, then let me say that I am so happy for you. True friends are hard to come by, and when you find them, they are truly a gift from Hashem. But just having good friends isn't enough; you need to nurture those friendships. Here's how:

1. *Show up*
I know I have raved countless times about how much I love WhatsApp, especially when I can use it to chat with my friends. However, I also believe that there is no substitute for in-person meetings when it comes to building strong friendships. Virtual connection is great for staying connected and holding down the fort when our lives get hectic, but there is a certain level of depth and authenticity that only real-life interactions can provide.

There's nothing like the experience of attending an event together. There's nothing like experiencing the subtleties of life together, like when you notice your friend eyeing that item on the shelf she doesn't need and you both crack up. Or you bump into interesting people, spill the coffee, and experience life together. Or you tear up when she's crying over her hurt. That tight hug when you meet or before you part. These are the moments that trigger a flood of endorphins and leave you feeling alive, loved, understood, and supported.

Making plans to meet up with friends can be tough, and it's easy to succumb to resistance. We all have busy lives, never-ending to-do lists, and anxiety that can hold us back from reaching out to our friends. Even I find myself wanting to cancel meet-ups from time to time. It's the craziest thing because I feel so young and alive after meeting my friend for coffee or going out at night. Yet I often find myself looking for reasons to cancel. Life is busy. I am busy! And I'm not starving for social stimulation. So when it comes to making arrangements for friendship events, it's at the expense of something else, and I often consider ditching it.

That's what we call resistance. Resistance is a party pooper who never wants you to go out and have fun with your friends. It's like that one friend who always says, "I'm too tired," or "I have to fold the laundry" when you invite her to a fun night out. Except in this case, the friend is you, and the party is your social life. Resistance is real. The better something is for us, the more resistance we will feel.

We have to learn to tell resistance to take a hike while you go join the party. I always try to remind myself of how good I'll feel afterward—it's always worth it! As I like to say, "If you think you can't afford the time to go out for an hour with a friend every two weeks, then you really can't afford not to!"

2. Express your gratitude

From time to time, show your friends how much you appreciate them.

It doesn't have to be anything grand. Sometimes a simple text can do the trick. If you vent to a friend and she listens actively, it shouldn't be hard to follow up with a message saying, "Thanks for listening! I feel better already." Or the next day, you can send a text saying, "By the way, I want to thank you for listening to me yesterday. It made me feel so much better. Thanks for always being there. It means a lot to me."

Gifts are another great way to show your appreciation. They don't have to be pricey; it's the thought that counts. I have a friend who is a master of long-distance relationships. Whenever there's a special occasion, whether it's my birthday or my son's *upsherin*, a cute toy or a thoughtful gift will show up at my door. Amazon Prime makes it so easy to send these heartwarming little gifts. I remember when I was pregnant and feeling super anxious, she sent me this adorable candle that said, "Mommy's last nerve, look! It's on fire!" along with a few kind words. I can't explain how much that gesture meant to me. It showed me that she really cared and that she had been listening.

3. Always support

Nurturing friendships involves wholeheartedly supporting your friends in their endeavors, including their business ventures. Whatever your friends do, you're there to cheer them on. If they open a business, you buy from them. Even if you can't purchase their product, your support can take many forms, such as spreading the word about their products or services, helping with marketing, reposting their ads, attending their events, and providing a listening ear during challenging times. Having a listening ear is one of the most valuable types of support I have received.

It's not just in business that we can support our friends. Support whatever your friend is involved in—a charity campaign, for example. Today's online fundraising campaigns turn us all into fundraisers, whether we want it or not. When our child's school creates a personal fundraising page with our name and a hefty goal, it can be uncomfortable, vulnerable, and challenging.

Despite constantly being bombarded by tzedakah links, which can spiral into feelings of obligation, resentment, and guilt, I've come to appreciate these campaigns for the opportunity they give me to show loyalty to the people who really matter in my life. I'm not talking about an ex-classmate or acquaintance who suddenly comes out of the woodwork with a link to donate to her son's yeshivah's campaign. I'm talking about my real friends. It's an opportunity to show my support in an easy way. It's not a cake I need to bake, a gift idea I have to brainstorm, or a birthday card I need to remember to mail; it's a link that lands in the palm of my hand, and all I need to do is click it and enter my credit card information.

Aside from the *sechar* (reward) you get by making a donation to a friend's page, it's a beautiful way of cultivating friendship and showing support. When someone I care about is fundraising, it really doesn't matter what the cause is or what connection I have to that particular organization. If I care about the person, I try to give something. It doesn't have to be a large amount. Any amount with a nice message tells your friend, "Whatever you do, I'm with you." It's the gesture that counts.

Finding True Friends

And that brings us to the million-dollar question: "This all sounds great, but where do I even begin? Where and how do I find these true friends?"

Are you feeling a little lost and wondering how to find these elusive friends? It's easy to feel isolated and unsure of how to make meaningful connections, especially as an adult in the big wide world.

I've got your back. Well, at least I'll give it my best shot and share whatever wisdom I've picked up along the way. Here is a list of things you can do to help make friends as an adult:

1. *Talk to Hashem*
First and foremost, pray! Ask Hashem to bring good friends into your life. Ask Hashem to guide you towards the right people as you light those Shabbos candles.

2. *Branch out to meet new people*
You may have friends already, but perhaps they're not the kind of friends you can confide in and share your deepest thoughts. Maybe you've never invested enough time or been vulnerable enough to take your relationships to the next level. If you're lucky enough to have wonderful people in your life or neighborhood, it might be worth deepening those existing relationships first. After all, the best friendships are often built on a

foundation of mutual trust and understanding. However, if your current social circle isn't quite cutting it, it's time to take action.

One great way to meet new people is by joining a class or club that aligns with your interests. If you're into personal growth and development, for example, you might consider enrolling in an in-person course or workshop. You're bound to encounter like-minded individuals who share your passion for self-improvement. If you're a parent, the local park or a mommy and me club could be a great way to connect with other mothers in your community. Not only will you have the chance to bond over the joys and challenges of motherhood, but your kids will also have the opportunity to make new friends—two for the price of one!

Of course, sometimes the best friendships are formed in unexpected places. Take, for instance, my experience at the Keiravtuni Shabbatons. I didn't attend these Shabbosim with the intention of making new friends, but that's exactly what happened. By being open to new experiences and opportunities, I was able to connect with people from all walks of life. I met one of my closest true friends from Monroe there!

Whether you're an introvert or an extrovert, whether you're shy or outgoing, attending social events and activities can be a powerful way to expand your social circle and build meaningful connections. If starting a conversation with a stranger feels as natural to you as trying to perform brain surgery, don't worry—you're not alone! But remember, even the most introverted among us can benefit from putting ourselves out there and striking up a conversation every now and then. Who knows, you might even surprise yourself and enjoy it! And if all else fails, just remember: fake it 'til you make it! By being open to new experiences, you never know who you might meet or what friendships you might form.

3. Be open-minded and embrace diversity in people
First and foremost, be open-minded! Friends can come from anywhere and be any age. Making new friends requires an open mind and a willingness to step outside your comfort zone.

While there is value in surrounding yourself with individuals who share your interests and background, it's also essential to challenge yourself and not limit yourself to people who are just like you. Being in a bubble where everyone is like you and agrees with you may be comfortable, but it doesn't provide an opportunity for growth.

As a person who grew up in a sheltered community, I'm well-acquainted with the belief held by some that making friends with those outside the community is risky. I believe this is a misguided notion. You may find that your values don't always align, but that's okay. Your values don't need to be shared, but they need to be respected. If your values are mocked in any way, if you feel shame in showing up as yourself because your values aren't respected, you need to rethink the relationship.

And I personally believe that it's not only great to have friends from different backgrounds, it's also essential. Having a diverse group of friends means you get to learn from individuals with different backgrounds and beliefs. This diversity can be the key to help us grow as humans. We can't learn or grow in an echo chamber of like-minded people. I discuss this more later, in the chapter "Open Hearts, Open Minds."

4. Be yourself and show your true personality
It can be intimidating to put yourself out there to try to make new friends, especially if you've had negative experiences in the past. Some women might feel like they need to present a perfect version of themselves to avoid being judged or criticized. However, this can be a slippery slope, as it can lead to a cycle of inauthenticity and superficial relationships.

Ultimately, it's important for women to recognize that their true selves are valuable and worthy of connection. By embracing their authentic personalities and being open to vulnerability, women can build meaningful relationships with others who appreciate them for who they truly are. Don't be afraid to show your true colors; speak your mind, and let your personality shine through.

Share your interests and passions with others. Your genuine nature is what will attract the right people to you and help you form meaningful connections that can last a lifetime. *Your* people will appreciate and celebrate you for exactly who you are. You want to attract those people.

5. Avoid being impulsive and rushing into friendships
This one is very important, and unfortunately, I learned this the hard way. Women can become desperate. When they find themselves drawn

to someone they meet, they may be tempted to dive headfirst into a new friendship without taking the time to get to know the person properly.

They may spend hours talking to this person, whether it is through social media, messaging, or in-person conversations. They talk non-stop for a few days. They may overshare because they think they clicked and have found "the one."

These impulsive connections very often fizzle out just as quickly as they started. The initial excitement wears off, and women may realize that they don't actually have that much in common, or they don't share the same interests. This realization can be disappointing and leave them feeling foolish for investing so much time and energy into a fleeting connection. That's why it's important to take the time to get to know someone before giving too much of yourself.

Rushing into a friendship based on initial attraction or convenience might provide temporary satisfaction, but it's unlikely to lead to a lasting and fulfilling relationship. It's important to be patient, actively listen, and share your thoughts and interests to build a connection. True friendships take time and effort to cultivate and are built on a foundation of trust and mutual respect. So if you find yourself caught up in an impulsive conversation, take a step back and evaluate the situation.

Remember, forming deep and meaningful friendships is a journey, not a race. Making friends is like embarking on a thrilling adventure filled with laughter, unforgettable moments, and yes, the occasional embarrassing blunder and cringe-worthy moments.

Gear up and embark on this friendship journey! Be unapologetically yourself, because the right people will love you for it. Embrace the nerves, for they're a sign that something wonderful is about to unfold. And through it all, keep that line of communication open with your Father in Heaven. He's always there with you, to guide you and shower you with blessings.

I'm here, cheering you on, and I wish you nothing but the best of friends! May you discover true, enriching, wholesome friendships that fill you up in the most impactful way. Special relationships that make you feel alive and make your heart sing, creating cherished memories and spawning inside jokes that will leave you laughing for years to come.

> "If you see what needs to be repaired and how to repair it, then you have found a piece of the world that G-d has left for you to complete. But if you only see what is wrong and ugly in the world, then it is yourself that needs repair."
>
> – The Lubavitcher Rebbe

NEBACH

"Y**OU HEARD?** *NEBACH!*"

Every recess in high school, day in and day out, my classmates would gather around the teacher's desk, eagerly sharing about other people's *tzarus* (tragedies) with as many details as they had, all while munching on their crispy snacks. Each contributed eagerly to this grand nebach-fest, their voices filled with thrill.

I couldn't stand it.

I wanted to scream, to preach, to give all my naive classmates a piece of my mind, but I remained silent. It was akin to those nightmares where you try to scream, yet no sound emerges. You find yourself on the streets in a nightgown, longing to escape but paralyzed in place. Have you ever experienced such a dream?

Okay, it's a good sign. I had so many of those as a teenager. Recently, I read somewhere that dreaming of being inappropriately dressed in public and unable to run signifies you're hiding something.

How true that was! I carried so many heavy secrets as a teenager—some that I still carry today.

People often perceive me as an open book because I share so much. But they'll never truly know the experiences that shaped me into the woman I am today.

I'm okay now. Because I do have my few close people in my life who now know. But back in school, *no one* knew...

I was in elementary school. It was one of those late-night moments at my then-best friend's house. A time when the usual daytime chatter fades into the background, replaced by deeper, more intimate conversations. As the night deepened, there was a palpable sense of intimacy, a feeling where the usual barriers melt away. Surrounded by the soft glow of the street lamps and the muffled sounds of the night outside, I felt an overwhelming urge to share. It was the moment—the perfect opportunity to reveal those secrets and thoughts that had been weighing on my mind.

"I want to tell you a big secret. But you promise you won't tell anyone?" I asked with a quivering voice.

"Sure," she said. But I wasn't convinced. I drove her crazy for the next twenty minutes, making her promise me in a million different ways. And once I exhausted every possible way for her to express how trustworthy she was, I didn't know what to do with myself. My friend was waiting with bated breath, but I was still too petrified to say the words out loud.

So, I pulled out my creativity. I said, "I was kidding!" I maneuvered my way out of the buildup by pretending it was all a big prank and that I didn't really have any secret to share.

She was mad, her frustration etched across her face, hanging heavy in the tense silence that followed. But I was even more frustrated.

Intense frustration, trapped in my own silence.

I was suffocated by my secrets. And I can still feel that horrible, bitter taste deep inside my throat. I went home, shoulders slumped ... defeated.

That's where I found myself throughout my school years. When I would overhear my classmates animatedly discussing everyone's troubles, moaning and sighing as if they truly cared, while in reality, relishing the drama—it made my blood boil. What did they know? They seemed oblivious to the depth of complexity and pain that some people endured.

This is a poem I wrote in tenth grade, born out of frustration from the ongoing lack of empathy around me.

NEBACH

>Someone's cousin lay sick in bed,
>"*Nebach! The family is hiding it, but I know.*"
>Another father of ten dead,
>"*Nebach! Look at his kids so alone.*"
>
>Someone's neighbor is sitting in jail,
>"*Nebach! His wife estranged.*"
>Another's son is a total fail,
>"*Nebach! The family has such shame.*"
>
>Someone's daughter is acting like a goy,
>"*Nebach! How can she act so?*"
>Another's sister just divorced, Oy!
>"*Nebach! For the parents, no?*"
>
>Someone's sibling is deadly ill,
>"*Nebach! Did they try surgery?*"
>Another's cousin is single still,
>"*Nebach! I heard they're picky.*"
>
>Remarks of "*Nebach!*"
>Are heard everywhere.
>And I'm listening and wondering,
>*Do they really care?*

That was me back then. In contrast, here's an Instagram post I wrote in 2021, following the Meron tragedy. The enormity of the tragedy was beyond our comprehension; everyone was struggling to process it, myself included. Questions of *emunah* (faith) were swirling in communal conversations and media as never before. It felt as if all the existential questions I had quietly wrestled with all my life were suddenly thrust into the spotlight, and it messed with my mind.

I experienced similar confusion during the communal challenges of the 2020 pandemic. I recall how people incessantly discussed what a tough year it had been, during and long after. They wrote that, "This year, we learned we are not in control." *Really?* I thought. *And until this year, you thought you were?* These were mature adults expressing their thoughts, and I found myself pondering repeatedly: was this really their first experience of helplessness?

Not to undermine anyone's experiences, but it triggered me. I'm not referring to those who lost loved ones, but those who were caught in the mayhem, fear, and uncertainty of quarantine.

It was challenging. But was this really the hardest thing these people had ever faced? Did they truly understand unending pain and helplessness? The kind where you witness unimaginable events and can't share with anyone?

At times, it felt like my weekly nightmares were more agonizing than months of lockdowns. I questioned if I was overreacting, if I was missing something.

I considered that perhaps these reflections weren't necessarily profound new realizations. Perhaps many were merely expressing common sentiments. This was something they could talk about openly, without risking their self-image. It was a shared pain, a communal experience, not personal or intimate. It was popular, trendy, and above all, safe.

And it was those thoughts that inspired this post:

> Once upon a time I was a naive little girl, trapped in a web of yentas and shame. Locked in a prison of paranoia, I didn't believe in the existence of empathy.
>
> Today, I *baruch Hashem* have real friends, with whom I can truly be myself. When I express pain, they don't raise eyebrows or ask questions. When I vent, they don't dwell. They understand the complexity of humanity and the greyness of this colorful life.

> I love being in my own world.
> A shapeless world, where humanity flows freely, like water between the rocks.
> Where personality and passion blow in the wind, throwing back kisses in your face.
>
> But then there's this mainstream world, where pain is wrapped in blankets of secrecy. Where *sheine mishpachahs* (nice families) carry their *peckel* (burdens) secretly. Where human experiences are crafted to be pleasing to the eye, while suffocating the soul.
>
> The communal grieving this week rocked my boat. Things got confusing. Lines blurred. Rules changed. Pain and questions were not only expressed publicly, but validated. The dam of fear burst, and human suffering flooded our nation. Streams of *chizuk* (strength) went viral. Klal Yisrael unanimously studied basic affirmations.
>
> I've realized that this grieving was not just about this tragedy. Humanity found a common, safe ground. Conversations came to light. This is something we can talk about, pain we can admit, hurt we can share...
>
> Suffocating souls came up for air, drinking up all they could get to quench their thirst. Bodies stuffed with suffering and pressure for so long exploded in a hiss of sobs and distress. It became blatantly obvious that more than 45 holy *neshamos* were being mourned...
>
> I yearn to yell it from the rooftops: there should never be shame for pain. No one should need to gobble up support in disproportionate doses. Mankind is filled with genuine individuals who will catch your tears and nod with compassion.
>
> Sister, the hearts and the *chizuk* are always needed, and always here. It's wired into the framework of our nation and *Yiddishkeit*. You just need to keep believing it exists, keep seeking it, and you'll find it.
>
> ♥Raizy

Over the years, I've observed that yentas exhibit several problematic behaviors. It's not just their nosiness and harmful gossip; it's also their tendency to sensationalize others' tragedies for their own entertainment. They seem disconnected, showing a troubling lack of compassion and understanding for the people they talk about. This behavior reveals a deeper issue: *a profound lack of empathy.*

Empathy is the ability to feel and understand the emotions of others as if they were your own. It involves genuinely connecting with another person's experience and responding with compassion. When you enthusiastically relay someone else's challenges, you broadcast to the world that you don't care. No amount of exaggerated sighs and dramatic "nebachs" can mask this lack of genuine concern. It's akin to adding LOL to a socially awkward text message—everyone knows it wasn't meant to be funny. Well, no matter how many "nebachs" you add after your detailed account, you still don't appear to have any *rachmanus* (compassion).

The same women who eagerly spread gossip across town often falter when confronted with real-life challenges, such as a loved one sharing that she experienced a miscarriage. They can recount misfortunes in detail to everyone, but when empathy is needed, they are at a loss. They stand blank, unable to offer the support required. They may resort to saying inappropriate things, asking invasive questions, or simply abandoning the person in need because they are unequipped with basic empathy skills.

To cultivate empathy, it's crucial to awaken your heart, engaging in active listening and mindful consideration of how your words and actions resonate with others. Listening to someone is an art—a crucial one, far beyond merely hearing their words. It's not just about uttering sympathetic sounds like "oh" and "ouch."

I worked on myself to become a better listener, to be there for others in the right way. Today, *baruch Hashem*, it comes naturally to me, but I definitely put in the effort. I recall vividly the times I would sit with others as they poured out their hearts, mentally coaching myself: "Don't look horrified, don't appear shocked, just look caring." This is the essence of genuine listening. Genuine listening requires not just your ears, but your entire being. The most disheartening experience is pouring out your soul to someone and being met with exaggerated reactions, as if your life was a sensationalized soap opera. When someone bares her heart to you, it's not to entertain; it's to unburden, to be truly understood.

In those moments, your presence should be palpable, your silence a sanctuary. Your eyes must convey, "I feel for you, I care," rather than, "OMG, this is crazy! This is so fascinating and entertaining." It's hard to give a step-by-step guide, as this work is intuitive, but here's a basic outline to demonstrate how to think and react empathetically:

Scenario: A Friend is Grieving

Step 1: Listen attentively: Allow your friend to express her feelings without interruption. Show that you are fully present by maintaining eye contact and nodding occasionally.

Step 2: Validate feelings: Acknowledge her pain by saying something like, "I can't imagine how hard this must be for you." Simple affirmations, such as, "I understand" or "That sounds really tough," can go a long way. Allow her to speak at her own pace. Sometimes, the silence between words is as significant as the words themselves.

Step 3: Offer support without solutions: Instead of offering unsolicited advice, *segulos*, or remedies, simply say, "I'm here for you. How can I support you?" Remember, your goal is to understand, not to fix the situation. Just knowing that someone genuinely listens and cares is enough to make a profound difference.

Always remember to *be present*. Be present, both physically and emotionally. Focus entirely on the person speaking, putting aside distractions. Offer a safe space for her to express herself. This might mean holding back your own emotions and reactions.

When someone close to you is in distress, if you don't know what to say, just listen! If she chooses to share, listen without interjecting or offering solutions unless she asks for advice. Your quiet presence and attentiveness can be more comforting than any words. No one needs your suggestions; they need your understanding and support. Empathy isn't about fixing someone else's problems—it's about showing that you care and are willing to share the emotional burden.

If you often find yourself at a loss for words and unsure how to support a loved one going through a challenge, I urge you to get the book *The Rabbit Listened*. It's a children's book with very few words, but it's the best book I've read on the topic of true empathy and holding space for another person. Get the book and read it again and again, until the words are imprinted on your heart forever.

(Hey, I actually just remembered that I read it on an episode of Inspired Living. You can watch me read the book there and see the illustrations, too! The episode is called "Gifting and Receiving." That episode has a very special place in my heart—it's filled with creative care gift ideas that you can give to someone going through a hard time.)

The way I personally learned empathy wasn't from a book. It was from my very special friends, who I am so fortunate to have in my life.

You see, my friends, the people with whom I can truly be myself, are women who look just like they are "supposed to." They match their children, make potato kugel and farfel—and they've also been to hell and back. The scars from the furnace are there, under their classy clothing. My friends, my people, understand the oxymoron of those very *mechubadige* (highly esteemed) dysfunctional homes. They understand all too well how warmth and abuse can coexist. My people see this pixelated world we live in, where all the black and white squares appear so grey that we can't judge or differentiate.

They modeled for me what empathy looks and feels like. They showed me they understand without uttering a word. They don't ask questions. They don't give *brachos* (blessings). They just listen and empathize. When I experienced the warmth and comfort they offered, I felt compelled to emulate that, to be that person for others.

Once you've felt the genuine comfort of empathy, you can listen deeply without judgment, and provide a safe space for others to share their feelings without feeling self-conscious or thinking about yourself all the time. This is not about you; it's about the person in pain who needs you to be there for her. When you've been fortunate enough to be on the receiving end of true empathy, you can offer a comforting presence that says, "I understand, and I'm here with you."

In extending this gift of empathy, you create an aura of kindness and compassion. By nurturing empathy in yourself and sharing it generously, you cast a soft and comforting light that envelops those around you. You create an atmosphere of understanding and acceptance, illuminating the world with a warm, gentle glow that uplifts hearts, heals souls, deepens relationships, and saves lives.

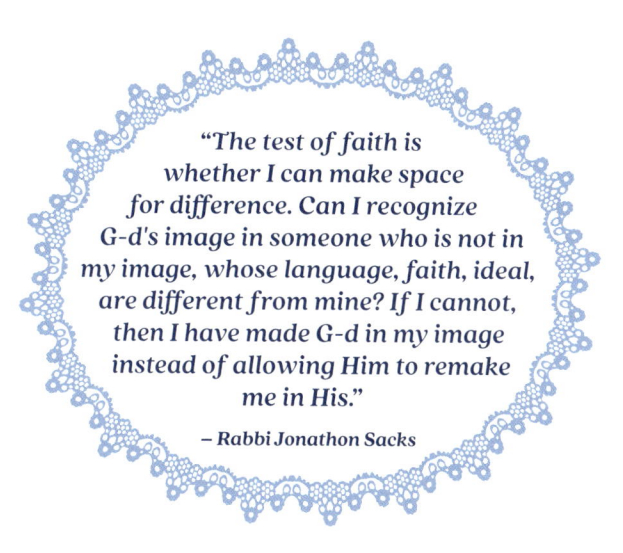

> "The test of faith is whether I can make space for difference. Can I recognize G-d's image in someone who is not in my image, whose language, faith, ideal, are different from mine? If I cannot, then I have made G-d in my image instead of allowing Him to remake me in His."
>
> – Rabbi Jonathon Sacks

OPEN HEARTS, OPEN MINDS

I WAS IN THE FINAL STRETCH OF PREGNANCY AND determined to conquer the world, despite physical and emotional exhaustion. I pushed myself to finish filming all the episodes for my show so I wouldn't have to schlep around in my ninth month and be able take a proper maternity break.

Everything seemed to be a struggle. The fatigue was taking a toll on me, both mentally and physically. Even with my best efforts to plan out my days, my body had other plans. Simple tasks such as answering emails, checking edits, and filming videos took so much out of me that I often found myself on the verge of tears. I would try to motivate myself, but the exhaustion was overwhelming.

It was as if my body and its hormones had taken on a life of their own, leaving me feeling helpless and out of control. Despite it all, I knew I had to push through. I couldn't let my fatigue get the best of me.

I felt a sense of overwhelm as I looked around at other mothers who seemed to be juggling so much more than me, with seemingly boundless energy and stamina. It had me perplexed, wondering—how? How do other mothers do it? I longed to have a large family, to experience the joy and chaos of raising many children. But how would I manage when it already felt like too much?

Not everyone has a job as intense as mine, but still, I see other mothers with way more kids than I have, somehow managing to keep everything running smoothly. The question kept nagging at me. How do other mothers manage to juggle so many responsibilities, to keep all those plates spinning without dropping a single one?

I knew that I needed a break—a chance to recharge my batteries and spend some quality time with my husband. But the thought of planning a full-blown vacation was too much to take on. So I turned to my go-to remedy: a weekend getaway in Monroe, New York to a place called Mei Menichas.

Mei Menichas is our little slice of heaven. It's a house-like secret getaway nestled in the heart of Monroe. It's far from glamorous; the house was originally built to be an orphanage, and later turned into a couples' getaway. It feels like your grandmother's house, without the grandmother. It's not luxurious—no fancy suites or extravagant meals—but that's exactly what we love about it.

Children aren't allowed. The atmosphere is discreet and private, with mostly ultra-*frum* guests who value modesty and *heimishness*. Many *rebbishe* couples go there, people who wouldn't feel comfortable eating in public. There is no communal dining room. At Mei Menichas, each couple eats their Shabbos meals in their simply furnished rooms next to the beds, around an old round table with two wooden chairs.

At Mei Menichas, you won't find any grandiose lobbies or bustling dining halls. The communal area is limited to a single living room with a handful of couches, and it's a rare sight to see couples occupying it—and on the off chance that there is a couple there, it's likely just my husband and me. There's an unspoken understanding that mingling isn't the norm at Mei Menichas. It's a place where modesty and privacy reign supreme, catering to the ultra-*frum* crowd who prefer to keep to themselves.

Because most of the guest are extremely *frum*, they don't have smartphones or social media access, and they don't know who I am. And that's the icing on the cake for me! It's a place where I can truly be comfortable, without the pressure to dress up, do the proper small talk or carry on with my public persona. I can lounge in my robe and tichel like a *kimpeturin* (woman recovering from childbirth), feeling relaxed and at home. The food may not be grandiose, but everything tastes *heimish*, delicious, and comforting.

Oh, great—now I've spilled the beans on our top-secret getaway that's been our little slice of heaven for years! But the fact is, Mei Menichas is not for everyone. If you're the kind of person who needs smorgasbords and fancy amenities, it's probably not your cup of tea anyway.

For my husband and me? It's like the Ritz Carlton, minus the crowds and fancy bellhops. So don't get any ideas about stealing our secret spot, okay? We need our *heimish* hideaway, where no one knows us, now more than ever!

Back to my story: I'm pregnant, overworked, and exhausted, and with what feels like my last bits of energy, I make the necessary calls. (Or rather, let's be totally honest here—I prefer using voice notes over old-fashioned phone calls, which, in my opinion, are a waste of time. Phone calls require a warm-up and a final chit-chat, since you can't just hang up the phone once you've received the answer to your question. Moreover, I believe that sending voice notes is a service to the person you're asking a favor from because they are not put on the spot and can take the time to think about it. From an efficiency standpoint, you can send your voice notes and know that they have been delivered. You don't have to play cat and mouse with people who are not at home or not available to pick up the phone. There are many more benefits to using WhatsApp over calling, and I could talk about it for hours. We may need a whole separate book for that.)

So, I send my voice notes, I sort out arrangements, divide the kids, and before I know it, I'm on the couch in Mei Menichas that Friday night, surrounded by some ladies.

I didn't come to socialize, but I needed a break from my room. So I sit with my *Mishpacha* magazine, ears piqued just in case something in the conversation catches my attention.

The conversation mostly revolves around Jewish geography, which isn't my kind of game. "*Dee bist Rechel Mariam's shneer? Ahhh!*" they exclaim. It's a group of women from Monroe and Tush, and I don't know any of them.

As I sit there, I overhear a few women talking about the recent weddings they have made and how they've come for Shabbos to rejuvenate after the wedding hustle.

"I just married off my ninth," exclaims a woman who looks so young. "But this one was actually easy. It was the first time I married off anyone while I wasn't pregnant, or with a small baby, or after a loss. For the other eight weddings, I was either pregnant, had a small baby, or had just suffered a loss."

The other women there were amazed. They had only married off one or three children, and they wanted to know how she managed to do it. "*Zug inz vee azoi dee tist dus*," they say. "Tell us how you do it."

As she continued to speak, she revealed that she had fourteen children. She shared the story of the wedding before this one, how she became pregnant with twins soon after the *shidduch*, but didn't take it seriously due to previous losses, including a loss of twins. It wasn't until a few months in, when she saw the babies weren't going anywhere, that she realized the pregnancy was for real and she had to go on bed rest.

She shared how Hashem helped her through it all and how it was still the nicest wedding ever, even if she had to return to bedrest immediately after the *chuppah*. She even joked about how everyone thought she had cancer because she wasn't showing yet, despite being in her seventh month.

As the woman spoke of her experiences with such ease and carefree joy, the other women sat with their mouths agape in astonishment, captivated by her story. "But how did you get ready for the wedding?" they asked, incredulous. "Who did everything?"

"I married off a son, not a daughter," she replied nonchalantly. "So what do we need already? A *bekeshe*? Some shirts? Everything can be delivered. I sent my children out."

The women were still astonished, unable to fathom how she had managed to pull it off so effortlessly. "But how can you not do anything with a houseful of kids?" they asked again, marveling at her seemingly carefree attitude towards such a monumental event.

"I just don't," she said calmly. "I have very complicated pregnancies. I've had many losses. My body basically prepares to give birth from the fifth month. Every time I'm pregnant, I have to be careful not to overexert myself, so I don't do anything. I just play lazy." The way she spoke about it made it seem as if it were the most natural thing in the world.

"You keep talking about your losses. How many losses did you have?" one woman asked her.

"A lot," she said. "About ten or eleven."

"Wow!" responded the woman who had asked. "I had five and I thought I had a lot."

I sat there listening from the side, feeling appalled. These women spoke about their experiences of loss as casually as I spoke about my lost umbrella. It was as if it was the most natural thing in the world. I didn't sense any hint of trauma or pain in their voices, just a matter-of-fact acceptance that loss was a part of life, much like getting your period.

Ironically, this all happened in the week following the release of an episode on *Inspired Living* on perinatal and infant loss, with Chumi Friedman and Yonina from A TIME. This attitude was a stark contrast to the emotional depth and rawness that I had addressed in the episode.

What followed was a lively conversation, swirling around the intricacies of juggling marriage, childbirth, triumphing over setbacks, and navigating a whirlwind of simultaneous events. These women openly shared their stories and how they pulled it off, with Hashem's help. Which had me thinking that maybe, just maybe, the age-old adage of *m'ken nisht tantze oif tzvei chassines oif a mul*, you can't dance at two weddings at a time, wasn't so accurate after all. These women seemed to be doing it effortlessly. Maybe we just need to upgrade our dance moves?

Now, I know what most women of my age and generation would think—that these women are crazy, martyrs, or numb. But that's not what I heard or felt from them. The conversation was refreshing, and I felt nothing but respect for them.

These women see life as it is. It's not just a walk in the park. They have a deep and genuine connection to the reality of life's ups and downs. While we often dwell over a miscarriage, they see it simply as a part of life. It was a different way of being, a different way of living.

I don't mean to disregard the importance and relevance of the episode I created or to dismiss the importance of awareness, education, and support for those suffering from pregnancy or infant loss. However, I realized that these women were truly blessed, and it was refreshing to hear their perspective.

In contrast to what most women of my generation may think, I don't believe these women are necessarily martyrs or unhealthy. They simply showcase a different way of living, one that emphasizes acceptance and resilience.

I envied them.

This woman with the fourteen children and ten losses was continuing to share. As she spoke, the manner in which she conveyed her beliefs was simple and unambiguous. With a matter-of-fact tone, she shared her conviction that Hashem provides assistance, whether one is pregnant or not, and that ultimately, we have no control over the outcome of events. Her words were straightforward and devoid of any pretense, and her unwavering belief that *Der Eibeshter shikt tzee* (Hashem sends what is meant to be) was evident in every sentence she uttered.

"Who took care of everything while you were on bedrest?" asked one of the women.

"Took care of what? What do you mean?" she asked in confusion.

"Like setting up the guest rooms and taking care of the welcome packages for the guests."

"*Uh dee machst peklach*—Oh! You make packages!" she exclaimed. Her expression shifted to a knowing look as she matter-of-factly uttered her next statement:

"*Oib dee machst peklech, shlepstee yenem's peklech … Eech mach nisht kan welcome packages. Der Eibeshter get deer koach tzi trugen daane peklech, oib dee vilst machen packlech far andere mentchen, shlepstee andere mentchen's peklech—hustee nisht kan koach*".

"If you make packages, you end up schlepping other people's packages … I don't make any welcome packages. The Eibeshter gives you the energy to carry your own packages. If you want to make packages for others, then you end up carrying their packages—you don't have the energy for that."

The woman's matter-of-fact response carried a subtle, knowing undertone. Her expression held a hint of amusement and confidence, as if she understood the implications behind the act of driving oneself crazy by making welcome packages. The simplicity with which she spoke carried a deep statement about self-imposed high expectations.

They continued to discuss their thoughts on how the younger generation doesn't take enough help. As an example, another woman suggested, "You can teach your cleaning lady to fold laundry before your *chasunah* (wedding), so you don't have to search and sift through the hamper looking for tights during the week of *sheva brachos*."

I sat there in disbelief. My cleaning lady officially does my laundry. I have fewer children than most of these women, and I'm not planning a wedding. Yet I feel drained and wonder how people with more on their plates handle it all.

How can one believe that these women are oppressed or fanatical, when they are so obviously blessed with amazing capabilities? They have such a pure outlook on life and approach challenges in a straightforward, uncomplicated manner, believing that *der Eibeshter get deech dee koichis*, Hashem gives you strength. How can people view them as ignorant baby-making machines who are suffering, when these women lead rich lives that are full of *nachas* and joy? They are well taken care of, healthier than I am, and overall happier individuals who are organically connected.

I used to be on the other side, judging and mocking these types of women, but now I see things differently.

I'll tell you this—I took the most liberal route to conservatism. So I know both extremes really well. I've come to realize that it's only when you can recognize this, that you can truly consider yourself open-minded.

Here's what I've learned: you know you've healed when you're able to see the other side. It doesn't mean you have to agree with it or even adopt it, but you can understand it and respect it. You can appreciate a different way of life, even if it's not something you see yourself doing. And perhaps most importantly, you recognize that everyone around you has an internal life that's just as complex and nuanced as yours.

We each come from different backgrounds and have experienced different extremes, which makes it impossible to issue blanket statements about anyone. Sometimes we see the ugly side of things up close, but ultimately, we are here on this earth to work on ourselves. Healing starts when we stop mocking others, blaming others, and take responsibility for our own lives. Only when we practice empathy and seek to understand where others come from, can we break the cycle of hurt and pain.

These women in Mei Menichas are content with their lives and show up for others without judgment. They are truly *gantz mit zeech*, whole and confident with who they are and their roles in life. Those are the women who, when you tell them about your hardships, won't judge. They will be compassionate. They will tell you to take more help and offer practical advice.

Because they are not hiding their own misery or pretending to be fine, they are not intimidated by others or triggered by the complaints of others, and can offer genuine compassion and practical advice.

I can only hope and strive to be like these remarkable women—to exude a genuine sense of calm, compassion, and resilience in everything I do. It's the ultimate goal of my life, and though I've come far, I know there is still much work to be done. But with their shining example before me, I know that anything is possible.

Curiosity and Acceptance

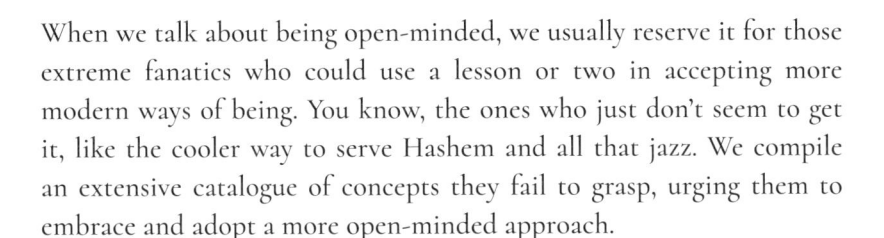

When we talk about being open-minded, we usually reserve it for those extreme fanatics who could use a lesson or two in accepting more modern ways of being. You know, the ones who just don't seem to get it, like the cooler way to serve Hashem and all that jazz. We compile an extensive catalogue of concepts they fail to grasp, urging them to embrace and adopt a more open-minded approach.

However, here's what I've noticed: the people who claim to be open-minded are often the most closed-minded folks out there. Open-minded is not about how cool you dress. It's about your state of mind, my friend. If you're quick to judge women who choose different lifestyles, whether they prefer a more sheltered life, have larger families, or dress more modestly, well, I hate to break it to you, but you're just as narrow minded as those you criticize!

So let's set the record straight and define what being open-minded really means, shall we?

Being open-minded isn't a fixed personality trait, something you're born with or without.

Open-mindedness is a state of mind, a way of thinking, where you are naturally willing to listen and consider other people's perspectives, even when they are quite different from your own. Open-mindedness is an attitude and unwavering readiness to embrace viewpoints even when they challenge our preconceived notions, values, and beliefs.

It's about not being stubborn, and having the patience, curiosity, and genuine desire to comprehend the intricate tapestry of another individual's worldview.

In the past, I used to argue quite a bit, passionately and fiercely sharing my opinions until I was flushed and red in the face. I was idealistic and naive, thinking that I could change the world by changing people's minds. I eventually realized that being stubborn and closed-minded was not cool. My attempts to change minds often turned into screeching matches that left me reeling long after the conversation was over. My mind would still be throbbing, racing with my strong opinions, face flushed as I lay on my pillow. Being idealistic did not feel cool.

It's true that some people argue with passion, but there is a fine line between passion and stubbornness. I've experienced many conversations where people repeat themselves without giving any consideration to opposing viewpoints, and it's frustrating and unproductive. It's sad when a conversation turns into a one-sided shouting match, and it's clear that some people lack the capacity to open their minds and try to understand where another person is coming from.

Over time, I have *baruch Hashem* changed my approach. I haven't become a lukewarm, mellow doll—I'm still extremely passionate and opinionated. But now, when faced with situations where others may not share my viewpoint, I become curious. I've delved into the fascinating world of emotions and understanding, seeking to learn from everyone I encounter.

It is possible to argue while maintaining an open mind, but it requires basic respect, a willingness to consider other perspectives, and being open to changing your opinion based on new evidence or arguments. I've come to understand that true open-mindedness involves actively seeking out and considering different perspectives, even if they contradict one's own beliefs or opinions. And it also involves being willing to admit when you are wrong, and making changes to your beliefs based on new information or experiences.

I've always been adventurous, and I've always had friends from all walks of life. My first job out of school was at a Syrian school, where I taught little six-year-old boys and girls. I was the only *chassidishe* girl there, surrounded by mostly Sephardi and Syrian colleagues, but I loved it. I enjoyed learning about their culture and broadening my horizons.

You know what I kept hearing while working at that job? "You're so normal!" I was the only *chassidishe* girl they had met, it seemed, and they were shocked at how normal I was. Even today I get that comment as one of the few *chassidishe* women who puts herself out there, in the public eye. I could have easily taken offense at that comment—why wouldn't I be normal? But I understand where they were coming from. Even though the Syrians I worked with came from a very different world than I did and were very cool and hip, I realized they were just as narrow-minded as many *chassidishe* women, or women from any other community, can be.

You know what's funny? I still remember when I first started sharing stories on Instagram. People would call me "Reizele" in this teasing, Yiddish-sounding way. Those self-proclaimed open-minded folks, with different backgrounds, would make fun of my *chassidishe* Boro Park accent. They'd comment on my pronunciation slip-ups, and let me tell you, it used to make me turn as red as a tomato. Seriously, it bothered me so much that I started Googling how to pronounce certain words before speaking them out loud.

But here's the ironic part that I didn't realize back then—who were these people to criticize me? I mean, how many languages do they speak fluently? One. Yep, you heard it right. They're masters of a single language, strutting around like they're the epitome of educated, while chassidim like me effortlessly read, write, and speak two languages fluently—Yiddish and English. Oh, and let's not forget, I and many others have a pretty solid command of Hebrew as well, so that's almost three languages. But back then, when my self-esteem wasn't as strong as it is today, I couldn't see it that way.

They wore longer wigs, and in my mind they were obviously cooler, more stylish, more educated, and more open-minded than me. I put them on a pedestal just like they did with themselves. Looking back, it's actually pretty funny now. Pathetic, but funny. And you know what? There are still some *chassidishe* women stuck in that mindset.

So if you're still in that place, this is me speaking directly to you: shake yourself out, straighten your back.

Last week I got a message that read, "How are you *chassidishe* and sooo normal! A true *kiddish Hashem*!"

I responded: "But why wouldn't I be normal? Thanks for the compliment, but it implies that it's a wonder that a *chassidishe* girl turned out normal, or that I'm out of the ordinary, and that's the furthest thing from the truth!"

To anyone thinking that, you need to learn more about us and meet more fabulous *chassidishe* women.

Encountering people from diverse backgrounds with an open mind and a receptive heart has undoubtedly played a significant role in shaping who I am today. However, I've come to realize that simply knowing more and understanding more does not make us better people. It only makes us *capable* of becoming better people.

You can't change other people, and you definitely can't fix their self-esteem issues. What you can do is work on your own self-esteem, recognize your incredible strengths, and yes, also strive to become more open-minded yourself. Regardless of our backgrounds, we can all put in the effort to open our minds a little bit more. Let's embrace our uniqueness, celebrate our strengths, and challenge ourselves to be more accepting and open-minded.

I've got a little list of some core strategies that can help you become more open-minded. Here it goes:

1. Avoid jumping to conclusions
Try to avoid making assumptions or judgments before you fully understand someone else's perspective. Resist the temptation to roll your eyes and instead, open yourself to the wonderful world of new insights and possibilities!

2. Embrace the curiosity bug
Let your inner inquisitive spirit shine! Show genuine interest in learning about new perspectives. Ask questions. Open-minded people tend to ask questions, rather than offer their own opinions or argue. You can practice asking more questions during almost any conversation. (But not too many! Be curious, but not in a way that sounds like an interrogation. Balance is key, my friend.)

3. Listen actively
Practice the art of active listening by putting your focus on what the other person is saying. No need to rush to give your opinion

or formulate your response. And hey, while we're at it, feel free to paraphrase here and there to ensure you understand and you've got the right picture. (But don't go overboard with it, because let's face it, nobody wants to feel like they're in a therapy session. Right?)

4. *Challenge those sneaky assumptions*
Be willing to question your own beliefs and opinions. Consider other points of view, and try to see things from different angles.

5. *Practice empathy*
Try to put yourself in someone else's shoes and understand their perspective. Show compassion and understanding, even if you don't agree with their opinions.

6. *Stay open to change*
Be willing to change your mind if presented with compelling evidence or arguments. Recognize that flexibility is not wishy-washy, but a strength! Be open with acknowledging that your opinions and beliefs can evolve over time.

Being more open-minded is like giving your brain a fantastic upgrade to OpenMindOS 2.0, the snazzy operating system that lets you navigate the vast world of diverse ideas and perspectives with ease. It's like swapping out your old mental two-wheeler baggage for a shiny set of neon-colored four-wheelers, ready to cruise through the highways of understanding and compassion.

But you know what? It's not just about improving your brain's functionality. More importantly—it's about becoming a better human and a better Yid, too! When you embrace open-mindedness, you become a master of *dan l'kaf zechus*, a non-judgmental champion, and a loving member of society.

Becoming more open-minded is a journey, not a destination. With these strategies in mind, we can all work towards being more understanding, accepting, and compassionate individuals. So let's throw open the doors of our minds and hearts, and watch in awe as the world becomes a brighter, more harmonious place.

> "Blaze your own path.
> You can be sure that it has not
> been sullied by others."
>
> – Rabbi Menachem Mendel of Kotzk

WHO DO YOU THINK YOU ARE?

ECH DAVEN AZ ES ZUL NISHT SHAATEN KEIN AYIN HURE *oif deer yeiden tug.* I pray every day that no evil eye should be inflicted on you," a dear relative recently shared with me. His voice carried a mixture of love and unease, a heartfelt concern that flowed like a gentle stream winding its way between rocks. I felt the protective currents of affection and ripples of worry in his words.

Despite his best intentions and the warmth in his heart, the words struck me cold, and my soul trembled.

I found myself at the crossroads of vulnerability and strength, a dichotomy of emotions that tugged at the corners of my consciousness. A whisper of doubt tiptoed into my thoughts, prompting me to ponder whether perhaps I was putting too much of myself out there on a platter for the world to see. The apprehension wrapped around me like a gentle mist, causing me to second-guess my willingness to stand boldly in the spotlight of my soul's mission.

In response to the gentle turmoil of doubt, a chorus of unyielding voices rose within me. A symphony of mentors and luminaries, woven through history, stood resolute against the tide. I thought about all these amazing people who've done incredible things, like the Belzer Rav, the Lubavitcher Rebbe, Sarah Schenirer, and even Dovid Hamelech from way back.

Imagine if they had held back because they were scared of the evil eye! What if they had hesitated under the shadow of the looming threat? What if they had chosen to diminish their radiance, cowering in the face of potential harm? Their collective wisdom reminded me that the pursuit of purpose requires unapologetic boldness.

That's all it took. I anchored myself in my mission. No need for worries. I knew what I was doing. I was on a mission, and I was in the right.

And all was good.

All was good, that is, until the devil visited.

You are surely familiar with him. He's that little troublemaker inside your head. Just when you think you've got a handle on things, he fills your mind with whispering doubts. And there's literally no escaping him. Because even when we realize he's got no basis for his claims and he's just here to drive us crazy and make our lives miserable, people will bring him up for you.

Who am I talking about? The "who-do-you-think-you-are" devil.

There I am, minding my own business, and this devil starts poking around in my thoughts. It's almost as if I can hear what people would say if they knew what I was thinking. And there we go again, another round of devil's advocate playing in my brain.

"Who do you think you are, comparing yourself to the Belzer Rav or Dovid Hamelech?"

"*Ver meinstee dee bist*, who do you think you are?" was my childhood companion. Wherever I went, it seemed everyone was bringing him up in conversations everywhere. I might not have a great memory, and I might not remember everything I learned in school, but the "who do you think you are" part of my *mesorah* is still deeply ingrained in me, and it always pipes up. I still fight it every day.

And here's something that truly grates on me: the way authority sometimes twists itself into knots. It's like a dance of contradictions that never fails to leave me shaking my head. You see, those very same folks who gasp at the unconventional side of me mustering the courage to blaze my own trail, to follow the example set by the great rabbis of history, are the ones who melt at the innocent words of a child expressing dreams of becoming the next *gadol hador*.

The accolades would pour in. "What a *tzaddikel!*" they'd exclaim, viewing these dreams as the embodiment of what a Yid should aspire to be.

What boggles my mind is this: when it suits their narrative, they want you to aim high, to reach for the stars and emulate our towering *gedolim*. Yet, should you dare to pull strength from the struggles and triumphs of these giants, should you dare to weave their lessons into your own mission to stand taller, suddenly they squirm in discomfort. For some unfathomable reason, they feel threatened.

"Who do you think you are?" they'll ask, as if the audacity to learn from our spiritual forebears is a transgression. They'd beam with pride if my son proclaimed he wanted to be like our *gedolim* when he grows up. But should they catch wind that I'm actually extracting strength from the adversity that these giants faced, it's like the access code has changed. Suddenly, it's not for me anymore. They want us to measure up to greatness—but only when it aligns with their predefined agenda and vision.

"*S'iz hechere zachen,* it's loftier things," they'll declare, like it's an inaccessible enigma. "*Vus farshteisti?* What do you understand?" It's a treasure meant for better, holier, smarter, bigger people. Not for you.

Listen, I won't sit here and pretend I've got a comprehensive handle on the vast expanse of wisdom that's out there. But here's what I do know. The Torah, from the forefathers and matriarchs to our revered *gedolim*, isn't a collection of tall tales to be read and shelved; it's a living guide, brimming with lessons waiting to be gleaned. It's a roadmap designed for us to navigate our existence, a source of strength we can draw from.

It's not a privilege reserved for a select few; it's an inheritance meant for all who seek its wisdom and inspiration.

> "Avraham and Yitzchok pass off their wives as their sisters, Yaacov deceives his blind father and takes his brother's blessing. Moshe loses his temper. Dovid commits adultery. Shlomo, wisest of all men, is led astray. The Torah hides none of this from us, and for a deeply consequential reason: to teach us that even the best are not perfect and even the worst are not devoid of merits. That is the best protection of our humanity."
>
> – Rabbi Jonathan Sacks, *Not in G-d's Name*

We gotta be on high alert for that sly devil, that "who-do-you-think-you-are" spirit, and all the underhanded tactics he pulls. Because if you want to use your talents and the precious gifts G-d has given you, if you want to fulfill your *tafkid*, you need to first recognize the devil to get past him.

Sometimes this devil shows up in your own voice. He's wearing a mask of your own thoughts, making you believe that these doubts are actually your own. It's a twisted game, trying to convince you that shrinking yourself is what you really want. He sneaks in, making you believe you're the one saying things like, "I'm not professional enough," or, "I'm too young."

And just when you start to catch on to his tricks, just when you're mustering the confidence to grow and expand into a bigger version of yourself, just when you're in the midst of creating something meaningful—he takes it up a notch. He morphs into this authoritative, seemingly well-intentioned figure, camouflaging himself in the Torah authority and teachings that should empower you the most.

Rabbi Moshe Chaim Luzzatto (the Ramchal), author of *Mesillas Yesharim*, which is studied in every yeshivah these days, was an outcast in his lifetime. He lived during a period when Kabbalists were persecuted, and his life was marked by tragedy. His books weren't merely overlooked; they were outright banned.

He found himself excommunicated on several occasions, first in his native Italy and then later in France. Seeking refuge, he fled to

Amsterdam, where he worked as a lens grinder. Yet even there, his adversaries relentlessly pursued him. Eventually, he emigrated to the land of Israel, only to meet his end in a cholera epidemic at the young age of 39.

Given all the adversity his work faced and his tragically short life, one might assume that his legacy would have faded into obscurity. But against all odds, history intervened and bestowed upon him a rehabilitation of sorts. This incredible transformation began in the wake of his passing, as his writings caught the attention and reverence of none other than the esteemed Vilna Gaon. It was a spark that ignited a fire of recognition, a fire that reached its pinnacle when his works were embraced as central pillars in the hallowed halls of *mussar yeshivos*, where the art of character refinement is paramount. Today, his teachings are cherished and studied and resonate as a timeless symphony that sweeps across the Jewish world.

These stories were once jolting in their revelations, yet they have now become an integral part of my understanding. They underscore the journey of the greatest minds among us, who have weathered their own storms of captivity and pursuit on diverse fronts.

If you study history, you'll notice a pattern that's both sad and inspiring. In the trajectory of every Jewish *gadol* who did something for the *klal*, it inevitably got nasty somewhere. No matter what goodness they did, someone accused them of transgressing. From the experiences of Dovid Hamelech to the profound teachings of the Ramchal, and, more recently, the Belzer Rav broadening the landscape of *kashrus*—most of our greats have experienced *asirim* and *redifah* on one level or another. Even the holiest of holies, Moshe Rabbeinu himself, faced accusations of immoral behavior by Korach and his followers.

Many people who suffered indignities in their lifetimes are only recognized and appreciated generations later. So first, recognize that if you're facing adversity, it often means nothing.

And if you think you're beyond all of this ... seriously? Who do you think you are? (insert winky emoji here). For there is no going around this. It's part of the territory. As the saying goes, "If you don't want anyone to talk negatively about you, don't say anything, do anything or be anything." That's your only solution.

According to Rabbi YY Jacobson, one of today's most significant challenges isn't necessarily about dealing with pure evil, negativity, self-centeredness, or even laziness. He believes that the greatest challenge we face in this generation is the lack of awareness of our inner wholeness. We are like ambassadors of infinity, carrying within us the potential for greatness. Yet too often, we succumb to the toxic voices that undermine our ability to truly shine as the individuals we are meant to be.

He claims that every generation has its unique challenges. It seems that in previous generations, people's egos were healthier. The Lubavitcher Rebbe said that the *yetzer hara* of this generation is four words: "*Mi ani, u'mah ani?* Who am I and what am I?" This encompasses all the negative thoughts of unworthiness. "Am I really capable? Who am I?"

I'm sure you've noticed that I frequently draw wisdom from the Lubavitcher Rebbe. This inclination is born from my profound connection to his teachings. What captivates me most is his remarkable ability to not just cultivate followers, but to nurture an entire generation of leaders. His foresight reached realms beyond our grasp, a visionary essence that continues to leave its imprint.

The Lubavitcher Rebbe stands as a potent antidote to the vexing whispers of the "who-do-you-think-you-are" devil that torment us internally. His legacy is one of empowerment, an invitation for every soul on this earth to dare, to become, and to share. His words reverberate profoundly: "If you know *aleph*, teach *aleph*." These words ignite a fire within, urging us to spread the light we possess even if it's just a spark of knowledge.

"If you know *aleph*, teach *aleph*" is a simple, profound statement that encapsulates his philosophy. It's an invitation to share whatever knowledge we possess, no matter how modest it may seem. You don't even need to know all the *aleph bais* to start teaching *aleph bais*. Armed with just a handful of letters, you can begin sharing knowledge and become a beacon of guidance for others. You don't need to be a master of all nuances to begin sharing the basics.

The recurring question that we heard growing up, "Who does she think she is?" echoes in tandem with our own self-doubt: "Who do I think I am?"

These questions often come from those who oppose our decision to use our voices. They're the individuals who feel uneasy about our choice to share knowledge, even if it's as modest as teaching *aleph*. It's a reflection of the monopolizing mentality that contradicts the essence of our soul's unique purpose on this earth. The notion of a monopoly stands in stark contrast to the core principles that our rich heritage teaches us; it contradicts the essence of *Yiddishkeit*.

So the next time that little devil whispers, "Who do you think you are?" just wink and say, "Someone awesome, obviously! Watch me shine!"

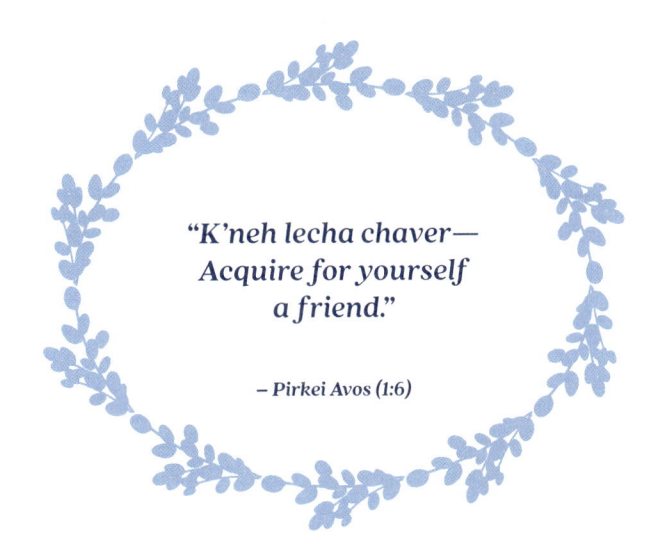

> "K'neh lecha chaver—
> Acquire for yourself
> a friend."
>
> – *Pirkei Avos (1:6)*

SHATTERED REFLECTIONS

Recently, I stumbled upon an intriguing interpretation of *"K'neh lecha chaver*—acquire for yourself a friend." According to the Arizal, the Hebrew word *k'neh* can also be understood as *kaneh*, meaning "quill." In other words, the advice can be rephrased as, "Let your quill be your friend." This suggests that our writing instrument can serve as our closest companion.

My pen (or the notes app on my phone) has always been my dearest confidant, especially during dark moments when friends were few and far between.

While most of my pieces will never see the light of day—just the dim glow of my phone screen—because they are too personal, too dark, too heavy... I have chosen a few that I feel comfortable sharing with the world.

This collection of poems delves into the pain of betrayal and broken trust, pieces of my broken heart pulled from my journal. They explore the loneliness and disappointment of strained friendships over the years. I share them in the hope that if you're experiencing similar struggles, you might find solace in knowing you're not alone. And to give you hope! For I am on the other side, *baruch Hashem*!

I wrote this after feeling completely drained by a friend who slipped out of my life when I wasn't looking, leaving me to suddenly find she was no longer there. I had truly believed we were close. It's hard to explain how deceived you feel when you've invested everything into a friendship, wrapped your heart in pretty paper and ribbon, and gifted it on every occasion. You push yourself to be there for someone, even when it's tough, only for her to disappear without explanation. One minute, she's there, and the next, she's gone. You keep reaching out, hoping for a response, only to realize you're chasing something that's no longer there. The crushing pain of feeling both confused and deceived is beyond words.

FRIEND-SHIFT

> She sucked out everything
> Then disappeared.
> It hurt.
> But I learned
> What I possess.
> The things
> I bring to the table.
> A likeable personality,
> Wisdom.
> It messed with my mind,
> But I learned
> Life is a Come and Go.
> There will always be noshers,
> And there's beauty in that.
> But when someone
> Devours the whole buffet,
> Emptying tray after tray...
> Licking all the plates dry.
> Then they go...
> Without clean-up, or a word.
> That's another story.
> A painful one.
> But I learned

That's part of growing.
I want to keep inviting,
Not to stop caring.
Not to stop trusting.
I'll just learn
How to balance it all in a way,
Where I enjoy my gifts every day.

During those friendless days, I longed for connection. When I met two geshmake women in my neighborhood, hope swelled within me. We hit it off, and together we eagerly planned a girls' night out. I could already picture one of them becoming a new friend. But as the evening dragged on, their shallow conversations and glaring lack of integrity became painfully obvious. Their standards were worlds apart from mine, and their attitudes... it soon became clear—this was not for me.

Returning home, I was utterly crushed, feeling as though I was back to square one. My family was already asleep, and in the quiet of the kitchen, I sat alone, overwhelmed by loneliness. As tears fell, I wrote the following poem with red and blue gel pens in my journal.

TURMOIL

Devastated by humanity
Lacking integrity

Solitary
Friendless
Lone existence

Pained
My heart
Shedding apart

Troubled
By humanity
Not for me.

Or is it me?

I wrote this poem years later, when I had acquired several close friends. Telling my younger self where life has taken me—the good and the bad—was healing, and gave me a fresh perspective. The Yiddish version poured out of me, a heartfelt stream of emotion and rhythm that felt like a natural extension of my soul. But then I decided to challenge myself and translate it into English. This was uncharted territory for me—translating poetry was something I had never done before. It quickly became an exhilarating puzzle, each line a game.

I found myself dancing between languages, sometimes rearranging verses to capture their essence in English, while at other times keeping it similar while preserving the original rhyme and flow. Hashem kept amazing me, dropping the perfect words in just the right lines—each one snapping into place like a piece fitting perfectly into its slot. I marveled at how similar these poems felt, each successful line as satisfying as clearing a row in Tetris.

For those who only know English, the translated poem captures the spirit and flow of the original Yiddish text. For those who are familiar with both languages, it might be cool for you to read both and see how the pieces of my puzzle fit together!

YOUNG RAIZY

Oh, if only you would see
What became of you—
That's me.

Things you never imagined
Even in your wildest dreams.
Much more than
A teacher or a scrapbooking queen.

Those dreams you had,
The things you longed to do—
All that and more,
It's all come true for you!

You live a life where
Creation is your art.
You bring ideas to life
From vision to start.

אינגע רייזי,

ווען נאָר דו וואָלסט געוואוסט...
וואָס איז געוואָרן מיט דיר,
וועמען הײנט דו ביסט.

וואָלסט זיך קײנמאָל נישט פֿאַרגעשטעלט,
ווי דײן חלום, אַסאַך בעסער
נישט קײן לערערין, נישט קײן אַרטיסט
אַסאַך גרעסער!

די חלומות וואָס דו האָסט געהאַט,
די זאַכן וואָס דו האָסט אַזוי געוואָלט טוהן...
דאָס אַלעס, און מער
מיט דײנע רצונות טוסט פליִען.

אַ סאָרט לעבן,
דײנע דמיונות-מאַכסט זײ געשעהן!
אײנס נאָך'ן אַנדערן,
פֿאַר יעדן צו זעהן.

It's not just talent,	ס'איז נישט בלויז געדאַנקען, און דמיונות,
Not merely a thought.	דו ווייסט,
You live your mission	און ערפילסט,
For which you've fought.	דיין תפקיד מיט דיינע כשרונות.
There was pain,	ס'איז געווען א בלוטיגע וועג,
Heartbreak, and strife.	מיט דיין נפש זיך אזוי פיל געראַנגלט,
But from that emerged	אבער האָסט געפונען חיות,
A brilliant light.	מיינונג, ליבע–דיין נשמה זיך ענטפאַנגלט.
But it's not all sunshine,	אבער ס'איז שווער,
Not only good happened.	נישט אלץ שטראַלט.
Some things became worse—	געוויסע זאכן,
Far worse than you could ever imagine.	איז ערגער געוואָרן, ביטער ווי גאַל.
A horror movie	ערגער ווי דיין–
Too painful to watch or bear.	שלעכסטע חלום,
Nightmares accompany.	שווער צו צו-זעהן,
But today, you can share.	שווער צו טראַכטן.
You can talk	אבער קענסט זיך העלפן,
Without quivering.	קענסט זיך היילן,
Your people know	האָסט נשמה מענטשן,
You're no longer shivering.	פאַר וועמען קענסט דערציילן.
They don't ask questions,	דו קענסט אויסשפּאַקן דיין האַרץ,
They're simply there.	אן טרייסלן.
Heartwarming energy,	דו קענסט מיטטיילן,
So much care.	אן ציטערן.
I know soul support	זיי פרעגן נישט קיין פראַגעס,
Is something you don't get,	זיי זענען פשוט דאָרט.
Well,	אמת'ע חבר'טעס,
Not yet…	א מתנה פון ג-ט.
It's coming soon,	זיי שפירן, זיי פארשטייען,
To keep you sane.	א ספּעציעלע קשר גאָר.
Deep-wired support,	איך ווייס, פאַרשטייסט נישט,
Bundled with the pain.	אָבער וועסט עס גוט פארשטיין–נאָך א פאָר יאָהר!!

Oh, and the best—	אוּן די בעסטע פֿון אַלעם,
How could I forget?	ווי אַזוי האָב איך פֿאַרגעסן?
Is your husband	איז דײַן מאַן!
Whom you haven't yet met!	וואָס האָסט נאָך נישט געטראָפֿן.
He's unique,	ער איז נישט אַזוי ווי דו שטעלסט זיך פֿאָר
Not what you might expect.	נאָר בעסער צוגעפּאַסט,
He's exactly what you need	פּונקטליך וואָס דו ברויכסט,
In every aspect.	אַלעס וואָס דו דאַרפֿסט.
He thinks the world of you.	ער האַלט פֿון דיר עולמות,
He lets you soar.	שטיצט דיר אויף יעדן טריט און שריט.
He stands behind	ער הערט דיר אויס,
Your visions, and all you strive for.	גייט מיט דיר מיט.
He listens	ער הערט אויס דײַנע געדאַנקן
To your thoughts and fantasies.	און דמיונות.
He supports your learning,	ער שטיצט דײַן לערנען,
Listens to your philosophies.	הערט אויס דײַנע תורות.
Yes, you're learning now.	יאָ, דו לערנסט תורה,
You keep craving more.	ס'קומט פֿון דיר אַליין...
The desire comes from deep	ביסט מחובר צו דײַן זעהל,
Within your core.	ביסט געקומען אַהיים.
You found your place in this world,	דו האָסט געטראָפֿן דײַן אָרט אינעם וועלט,
Your *neshamah* you see.	דײַן נשמה האָסטו אינזינען,
You nurture her well	פֿיטערסט איר,
With all that she needs.	מיט אַלעס וואָס זי דאַרף באַקומען.
Go, young Raizy,	גיי, אינגע רייזי,
Keep going in stride.	שפּאַן פֿאָרויס טריט נאָך טריט...
Just stay strong—	האַלט דיך שטאַרק,
You're in for a wonderful ride.	דו וועסט זעהן אַז ס'וועט דיר זײַן גאָר גוט.

Here's another piece that doesn't rhyme, because I didn't even try. It was one of those nights when I poured my heart out to Hashem, pleading with every ounce of my soul. I'm sharing this with you in the hope that it touches you and encourages you to connect with Him in your own way. Write, talk, sing, shout—whatever feels right. Just reach out!

Tatte in Himmel,
Please don't forsake us.
Even though I know You won't.
Please don't make us feel abandoned.
Who if not You, knows how much that feeling hurts.

I believe in You.
I believe You won't leave us.
I believe You hold us tight,
That's why I want to feel it.
Always.

When I watch horrific things,
It's very hard for me.
So many precious souls wilt away...

Watching, while my hands are tied...
Watching, while trying to continue living, loving, and laughing... Because life is good.

Yes, life is good, despite it all.
The traumas we keep on experiencing...
They remind us how fragile and beautiful life really is.

But it's hard, oh so painfully hard.
Watching and caring.
Coping and living.
Loving and thriving.
Thinking and breathing.

I don't need to understand.
I know I never truly will.
Yet I need help.
I need help passing things onto Your shoulders, *Tatte.*

I need help being there for my husband and children, at the times when it feels unbearable to exist.
I need help being a fortress.
I need help answering innocent questions that trigger and shatter my heart to smithereens.

I need help tip-toeing.
I need help explaining.
I need help teaching the things that took me so long to learn.
That bad things can happen to good people.
And it happens.

I need help figuring out how to tell them all this in a way they can understand, without being overwhelmed...
I need help guiding them through the greyness of life.
I need help answering their queries,
without breaking down in tears...
I need help preaching what's right, while I'm conflicted by the very same issues...

Tatte, please help me, and all those who don't have the *koach* to help themselves, to seek You, to find You, to take strength from You.

Those who don't have the *koach* to connect on a deeper level, and therefore go around suffering in silence, missing out on their precious life.

Help me.
Not because I'm special or deserving...
Simply as a *matnas chinum* (free gift)
Just because I know You can.

Help me.
And all those suffering, yesterday, today, and tomorrow.

Help me.
Because only You have, and only You can.

עד הנה עזרונו רחמיך
ולא עזבונו חסדיך
ואל תטשינו ה' אלוקינו לנצח
אני, 🖤
חיה ריזל בת בילא

Raizy Fried
inspired living

A VIDEO PLATFORM THAT WILL EDUCATE AND INSPIRE YOU TO LIVE YOUR BEST LIFE AS A JEWISH WOMAN.

Inspired Living is a haven of inspiration and wisdom, enriching every aspect of a Jewish woman's life. It's crafted exclusively for the woman who seeks more from life.

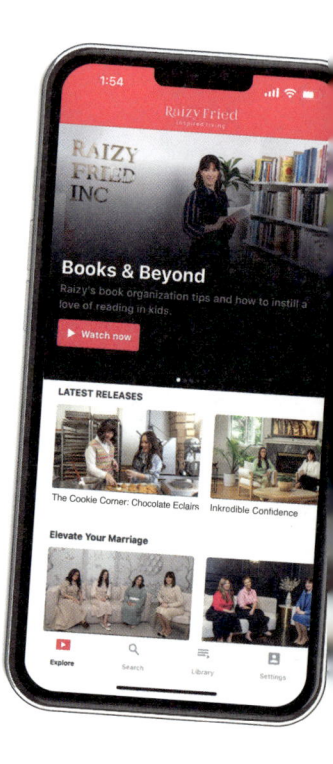

- Marriage
- Motherhood
- Self Growth
- Self Esteem
- Business & Being
- Creativity
- Homemaking
- Hosting
- Time Management
- Nurture Your Soul
- Culinary Skills & Tips
- Home Organization
- Conquering Challenges

Access a full library of episodes. Unlimited streaming. Fresh new video every Tuesday.

WATCH.RAIZYFRIED.COM OR DOWNLOAD THE RAIZY FRIED APP

GET IT ON Google Play
Download on the App Store

SCAN TO GET THE APP

Reviews from women just like you:

> It's not like watching a lecture; it's intimate, and you feel like a fly on the wall watching these animated conversations with the most incredible women. Raizy has an amazing, down-to-earth, and relatable way of promoting the inside information from our Torah.

> I am blown away by the content and the sophistication! A whole new level that's long been needed.

> Tuesday is the highlight of my week. Inspired Living is a platform vibrating with heart and soul. Such good supportive feminine energy. It gives me so much chizuk; it never ceases to amaze me.

> Each video is so special, so informative! I learned so much! Raizy opened my eyes to so many things, and I'm loving it!

> Raizy is exceptionally talented and open-minded and gets all topics! Raizy features such special women, I feel privileged to have the opportunity to 'meet' and learn from them. And she does it again and again weekly. It's like a dream come true for us Yiddishe mums... spot on knowledge, and we are learning so much!

> These videos are life-changing! It's very empowering as a mother to hear such positive messages.

> The Motherhood and Marriage sections are filled with real talk, no sugar-coating. Hearing from people like you that it's normal and we all adjust is HUGE.

> This is truly what we women need right now.

> I resonate with so many topics, especially those about creativity and the real struggles of motherhood and Yiddishkeit.

> I feel like this platform is tailored especially for me. It covers the topics we need to hear. This is not teen material.

> I love the very real, honest conversations about the challenges of motherhood. It often moves me to tears but then rejuvenates and fills me up, giving me strength for another day.

> I've been an Inspired Living subscriber since its inception, and it's just beyond, beyond. I look forward to every new episode on Tuesday, and it never disappoints.

> I look forward to Tuesday. I sit down for some quiet time with my coffee and watch the new episode.

Also Available from Raizy Fried

The ultimate Shabbos-prep handbook, *Lekoved Shabbos Kodesh* tells you everything you need to prepare a beautiful Shabbos.

Filled with practical tips, Raizy's favorite *heimishe* Shabbos recipes for every meal, sophisticated tablescapes, flower arranging tips, and uplifting stories, this is a special book for every Jewish woman who yearns to achieve true *oneg Shabbos*.

A creative masterpiece. This book will warm your heart, tickle your imagination, and stimulate your soul.

Raizy welcomes her readers into her world, sharing personal stories and imparting the wisdom she so needed to hear growing up. From young to old, you'll enjoy every moment immersed in this heartwarming book, as you discover how to create the sweetest Shabbos, week after week.

You'll learn how to:
- Accept your personality and embrace your creativity
- Create a truly *geshmake* Shabbos with love and care
- Set your Shabbos table with step-by-step napkin folding ideas
- Whip up easy dessert recipes
- Prepare homemade treats you'll be proud of
- Bake all sorts of cupcakes, cookies, and pastries
- Decorate fun Parsha Projects with sweets and nosh

Available at www.RaizyFried.com